Interpreting DREAMS

for Self Discovery

Collected essays edited by
Dr. Laurel Clark
&
Paul Blosser

SOM Publishing
Windyville, Missouri 65783 U.S.A.

Additional titles on dreams
The Dreamer's Dictionary
The Bible Interpreted in Dream Symbols
Understanding Your Dreams

soon to be released
Every Dream is about the Dreamer
What Teenagers Dream about
     & What it Means

© October, 2001
by the School of Metaphysics No. 100171

Cover Art by Sharka Glet
Cover Design by Patrick Andries

ISBN: 0-944386-25-3
Library of Congress Catalogue Number pending

PRINTED IN THE UNITED STATES OF AMERICA

If you desire to learn more about the research and
teachings in this book, write to School of Metaphysics
World Headquarters, Windyville, Missouri 65783.
Or call us at 417-345-8411.
Visit us on the Internet at www.som.org

Since 1973,
we at the School of Metaphysics (SOM)
have taught thousands of people
how to interpret dreams for self awareness.
Based on research which supports the existence of
a Universal Language of Mind,
SOM's dream education transforms lives.

The collective experience of the authors of these essays
spans 120 years of teaching and interpreting dreams
for people around the globe.
Dreams are both personal and universal.
They tell us as a planet we are in the midst
of constant change, often unconscious of the cause
or where the change will lead. They also tell us that
we desire harmony with ourselves and with each other,
and that we possess the qualities necessary to create
anything we imagine. They tell us that we are
experiencing in increasing numbers the limitless
dimensions of consciousness beyond the physical
world, and in that way these dreams give us a preview
of what is to come.

Everyone dreams every night.
By learning to interpret dreams, we can discover
a deeper meaning to our lives and a greater connection
with our fellow human beings.

The Contents

Foreword

Dreaming has always fascinated me. I can remember being a young child, curious and excited when I could remain awake as I entered the dreamland. Sometimes it felt like I was on a train, or going down a slide. I would slip into the realm of sleep, feeling myself being drawn into a tunnel and whoosh! into a dream. It didn't happen every night, but when it did, I knew there was a world beyond my waking life that was uplifting and exhilarating.

Although I didn't know the meaning of my dreams, I did believe that they were important. Oftentimes the memory of a dream would linger for days, even weeks, afterwards. It was as if the experience were still alive, and I wondered why.

I first began recording my dreams in college. I was taking a creative writing class, and one of my classmates wrote beautiful poetry. I was envious, and asked her how she came up with such vivid imagery.

"From my dreams!" she said. By that time I had learned to forget my dreams, and the few I remembered were usually nightmares, not ones that I was eager to write about.

"How do you remember them?" I asked her.

"It's simple," she told me. "Just get a journal and put it by your bed and start writing them down when you wake up.

You'll be surprised, just by deciding you want to write them down you'll start remembering your dreams."

I was a little skeptical, but decided to try it out. I already kept a journal in which I loved to write, and a friend had given me a blank book for a gift, so I decided to use that one just for recording dreams. I put it by my bed, told myself before going to sleep that I wanted to remember my dreams, and lo and behold, I did! I woke up with the faint echo of a dream in my consciousness, reached for my book and began scribbling. As I wrote down what I remembered, more and more of the dream appeared to me and poured out through my pen. As my friend had predicted, I was soon remembering most of my dreams, oftentimes not only one dream but several dreams in one night.

I still didn't know what the dreams meant, but I was curious about them. Some seemed very significant but I didn't know why. Others were frightening, nightmares that plagued me for days. When a friend introduced me to the School of Metaphysics, I rejoiced to find out the first night of class that we were going to learn to interpret our dreams. By that time I had filled two journals with dreams that I was avidly remembering and recording.

Learning to interpret dreams has changed my life. It has given me a way to reason with feelings that would otherwise be compulsive "gut instinct." It has enabled me to discern the lessons my soul needs to learn, to understand the meaning of my life experiences. Learning the Universal Language of Mind that dreams use for communication has brought me into conscious connection with my soul.

Dreams come from our subconscious mind, the inner mind that stores Universal Truth. Interpreting dreams opens a door into this Truth so that we can live accordingly. When we listen to these inner messages, it is like having a guide or a teacher sitting on our bed as we wake up, giving us a pat on the back for decisions well made, providing insight into the learning opportunities available in our waking life, offering a nudge or a way to direct our thinking in productive ways. As it says in the Bible, "Ye shall know the Truth and the Truth shall set you free."

This book grew out of a class assignment for a group of teachers teaching teachers in the School of Metaphysics. It reflects many different ways of thinking, showing both the universal character of dreams and the individual application of this eternal knowledge. Personal and practical, it can be helpful for teenagers and adults, parents and teachers, counselors and ministers.

Everyone dreams. When everyone knows how to interpret his or her dreams for self awareness, what a different world it will be! We welcome you on this journey of self discovery.

Dr. Laurel Clark
College of Metaphysics
September 2001

Introduction

A new language is necessary for a new age, a new time period. The enlightened person understands the language of the soul which is the language of the Subconscious Mind. Dreams have been studied throughout recorded history and before recorded history. In the past most thought dreams were referring to some outside event or other person. Dreams were taken as literal in many cases. Even when viewed as symbolic they were interpreted as something outside the dreamer such as an event to occur in some future time.

Through research spanning over a quarter of a century and tens of thousands of people-dreamers, the institute known as the School of Metaphysics has developed and taught the meaning of dreams. The symbolical language has been deciphered and is now available to all.

The intuitive and reasoning research has been done. The results are in. The results are herein published by the School of Metaphysics to be shared with the world.

This book is a compilation. Each chapter has been written by a different author. These authors are instructors and researchers in the School of Metaphysics, a not-for-profit educational and service institute. Most of these authors have ten or more years experience. Some have over twenty years experience in interpreting dreams, in teaching students and the public to learn to do the same.

This subject matter can be used by the professional and lay person alike as a reference manual on dreams and their meanings. It also will open the mind of the readers to vast untapped resources of their own minds which they can learn to use to create greater fulfillment in life.

The dream subjects in this book range from interpreting meanings of dreams to pre-cognitive dreams to healing dreams. From the practical application to the knowledge and wisdom contained in this volume each person can come to understand not only the meaning of life but also his or her purpose in life. This can be achieved by understanding the messages from their subconscious minds portrayed nightly in the form of dreams.

All too often the understanding of dreams is left out of the curriculum of schools, be they public or private. In fact, dream interpretation is not taught, covered or understood in most schools, institutes or ashrams of soul growth and spiritual development. Yet dream interpretation is of vital importance for anyone desiring to know Self. The dreamer's dreams, which come from subconscious mind, give honest, factual feedback about the individual's thoughts, attitudes and consciousness as the person was going through their daily activity.

The Subconscious Mind or soul, being older and wiser than the conscious mind, also gives wise and honest counsel for the student desiring to understand and master all of Mind.

Learn how dreams can be used as a practical mental tool, a valuable and beautiful way to understand yourself and your mind to find purpose, fulfillment and joy in life. Your light, love, truth, understanding and connectedness with all life will grow and expand. You will come to know the truth and the truth will set you free. I congratulate all the authors of this book and the people who have made it possible for they have done a great service in raising the consciousness of the people who make up humanity and in aiding the evolving consciousness of planet Earth.

Dr. Daniel Condron, D.M., D.D., M.S.
Chancellor, College of Metaphysics

Spiritual Dreaming

by Dr. Laurel Clark

Dreams are mystical and magical, mysterious and compelling. In the Bible, Joseph won the favor of a king by interpreting his dream. Shakespeare wrote of dreams so powerful they changed the course of his protagonists' lives. Inspiration, illumination, and inventions come from dreams. In our dreams we are poetic, musical, lyrical, and graceful. Dreams can also introduce us to the psychic realm. People have been known to dream the same dream simultaneously or to know what's happening on the other side of the world through a dream. Dreams can foretell the future. Past lifetimes can surface in dreams. Nightmares haunt us. Some dreams are so profound we remember them for our whole lives. These nighttime phenomena fascinate us because they link us with the supernatural, invisible world of the spirit.

I walked over to the flower bed with Hezekiah (a four-year-old boy). I was amazed to see that the bulbs I' d planted just the other day had grown huge sprouts already. They were about 6" tall. I reached into the dirt, feeling its richness in my hands, and said to Hezekiah, "Watering them every day really does make them grow, like your Daddy says."

I awakened from this dream with a deep sense of peace, exhilarated, and filled with well-being. It was as if I was centered in the awareness that all is right with the world. I used to experience this kind of well-being from remembering dreams even before I knew how to interpret them. Some dreams seem to radiate a supernatural quality and bring joy with them. Knowing that we exist beyond the physical world, that we have a connection with a higher reality, is, in itself, a nourishing experience. We can taste the thrill of contact with the divine through our dreams.

Now, knowing how to interpret dreams, I am able to glean greater insight from these ethereal happenings. This dream came during a period in my life when I was struggling with sadness and grief. My husband, whom I love very much, has diabetes and associated complications—blindness, kidney failure, extremely high blood pressure. Often the stress of his illness weighs heavily on my mind as I try to be loving, nurturing, and healing without fostering dependency and weakness. Much of my own learning in this experience revolves around understanding what love is, how to be creative and loving without attachment. Sometimes I make choices that come from my own fear of loss rather than from true love; other times I am more centered in the clear awareness of what is in John's best interest as a soul. I pray daily for understanding; i.e., for both of us to use this experience for our own soul growth.

When I got married, the "seed idea" for my marriage was that I wanted to learn to love as God loves. The dream was a kind of "pat on the back," telling me that this seed was growing and flourishing, *watered* by my life experiences. The *child*, a new idea or new way of life, was four years old, showing that this idea is not brand new but one that I have been cultivating for a little while. *Hands* symbolize purpose, and *soil* is the substance of the subconscious mind. When I *felt the rich soil in my hands* this shows that I am using these experiences for the purpose of producing soul growth. Furthermore, *Hezekiah's Daddy* is an aspect of my superconscious mind, my own Divine Self. Following the direction of the High Self brings peace because the superconscious mind holds our plan for existence.

We may think that a peaceful existence means one without conflict, but in fact, peace comes from understanding. Life is motion, change, growth, creation, and learning. When we attune ourselves to the rhythm of life and embrace learning and change, we are fulfilled. Dreaming is a continual way to be in contact with this inner reality. From our dreams we can learn to view our waking lives from a different perspective. What seems pleasant or unpleasant, easy or hard, good or bad to the conscious mind, is simply an experience to learn from the subconscious mind's perspective. We may not always *like* what we experience, but it is always perfect for what we need and want to learn. As we align our conscious mind with this subconscious objectivity, we become joyful. We appreciate every experience in life for the learning it offers; as it says in Psalm 118:24 , "This is the day the Lord has made, let us rejoice and be glad in it."

I was with a group of people who were celebrating a holiday like May Day. We were all dancing around in a circle. We were dancing a ritualistic dance, our hands up in the air. It was a dance to celebrate death.

This dream carried with it the feeling that it was very profound. I was energized and excited when I woke up, and I told everyone about it. My non-metaphysical companions thought I was a little strange to be celebrating death, but by the time I had the dream I had become a beginning student in metaphysics and I knew what the dream meant. *Death* in a dream symbolizes change. *May Day* is the beginning of spring, symbolizing growth and new life. *Hands* symbolize purpose. This dream occurred shortly after I had learned to meditate and I was meditating twice a day. The process of stilling my mind with concentration and listening to my inner Self through meditation was bringing about many beneficial changes in mySelf. I was beginning to align my consciousness with a deeper truth and to shed some of my unproductive habits. I was becoming aware of my true nature as a spiritual being, and my soul was rejoicing in these changes! What brings you joy? The birth of a child, a breathtaking sunset, raising your voice in song with a choir, a deep meditation... anything that connects you with something greater than yourself. Most people have some idea that life should be happy, but many people experience true joy only on rare occasions. Why? Because they exist by habit rather than giving purposeful direction to their life with spiritual ideals. The following dream illustrates this:

I was in my grandmother's house and I wanted to go up to the attic because I knew that my grandmother had a chest up there with beautiful, valuable things in it. As I started to go up the stairs to the attic, there was a dog on the steps and I stopped to play with it because it was so cute and cuddly. I never made it up to the attic.

A *house* in a dream symbolizes your mind. The *attic* is your superconscious mind, your inner divinity, and *grandmother* is an aspect of the highest part of your mind. This dream was telling the dreamer that she wanted to reach the highest part of her mind because she knew how valuable it was, but she was attached to some habit that kept her from it. When the woman heard this interpretation, she turned red. She had a habit of throwing temper tantrums and blaming people in positions of authority (like her boss) when she was expected to assume greater responsibility herself. The habit of blame was keeping her from realizing her highest potential. When the dream was interpreted, the woman began looking for ways she could use her daily experiences to mature, thus fulfilling her inner urge for progression and learning.

All of our experiences can be viewed as life lessons, because our life is a schoolroom designed for us to grow and become compatible with our Maker. By learning to interpret dreams, we can more readily understand the meaning of our life experiences, and this makes them rewarding.

Without the perspective that life is for learning, activity can become boring or seemingly unpleasant. If you listen to some people talk on the bus, at work, or on television, often their conversation is full of complaints about what is wrong with their life, with their job, their marriage, their health, the weather, the government, the economy, or something else. Often times they become dull or depressed, wondering why they should even get up in the morning, or "making it through" the work week to escape on the weekend. The following dream is fairly common for adults who have this kind of attitude:

I was back in high school, wandering the halls, looking for my classroom. When I finally found it, I discovered there was a test and I had not studied for it, nor had I attended the class all semester. I woke up sweating and frightened.

A *school* symbolizes a place for learning. This dream is telling the dreamer that he is missing out on the lessons that life holds for him, which is a frightful way to live! A purposeful life is one which centers around learning and feeding your soul with understanding. Most people believe that there is a purpose for life, some reason for being on this earth. Many people, however, do not know what this purpose is and crave inner fulfillment. What gives your life purpose? Having a good job, making good money, raising a family? Helping your neighbors? It is not the activity itself that is fulfilling; the fulfillment comes from giving of yourself.

Sometimes, even when engaged in worthwhile activities, people become bored or look for a new stimulus. This occurs when they live with physical goals and activity without a spiritual purpose. For many people, life is a physical game — working to make money to satisfy physical needs like food, clothing or shelter, trying to fill an inner void by accumulating material possessions that lose their appeal after awhile, looking for emotional comfort or sensory gratification in relationships, searching for a sense of satisfaction in building a reputation or being liked by other people. This kind of activity is frustrating because it feeds the physical, sensory self or conscious ego only. The excitement and stimulation is temporary. After it wears off, the hunger for a deeper meaning in life remains.

Dreams can be a great asset in helping you know how to live a purposeful existence, because your inner Self knows what your soul needs. Each of us has a dharma, a purpose in life, a destiny that gives our lives meaning when we fulfill it. Lifetime after lifetime we build understandings which become a permanent part of our soul, and there is an ever-present urge to give from this inner wealth of understandings. When we are giving, we are joyful. When we are in alignment with this soul urge, we love what we do and live a fulfilling life. As you give, you become. You can determine how you want to develop yourself — becoming more loving, kind, generous, determined, and so forth. This kind of direction gives you purpose. It enables you to look forward to each day, with the wonder and awe and reverence of a child coupled with the maturity and confidence of an adult.

I dreamed I was sitting in a car and all of a sudden I noticed my engagement ring was missing. Then I remembered that I had pulled it off my left hand and thrown it away after a fight with my fiance. I was sad until I heard a voice saying, "Don't worry, look at this one!" I looked down at my right hand and on it was an exquisite gold band that was much more precious than the one I'd thrown away.

I had this dream at a time in my life that seemed fraught with dramatic events. I had impulsively planned to get married, and at the last minute decided that the mate I'd chosen was a poor choice and my reasons for getting married were rather physical. Originally, I thought that this marriage would help me develop deeper communication and to become more expressive and open. This, I reasoned, would make me a better person and a better teacher. But I had gotten swept up in the physical marriage plans and was getting distracted from my purpose to be more communicative. I decided to cancel the wedding so that I could focus on teaching and helping other people. Although I was sure it was the right choice, I was still emotional about the decision. A *ring* in a dream symbolizes commitment, and this dream was telling me that I was moving from making physical commitments (the choice to be mated physically) to committing myself to awareness and spiritual development. The *ring on the right hand* symbolizes my commitment to spiritual development. This dream left me with a feeling of great awe, showing me that the thrill of aligning my mind with a greater plan transcends any temporary discomfort of emotional attachment.

Living a joyful life is a sure sign that you are filled with the presence of God, that you are connected with your soul. It doesn't cost any money, it's not difficult to attain; and it's with you all the time. Your soul is your inner self. It's the "you" that is eternal, that lasts beyond the physical body. It lasts beyond the ups and downs of everyday life. It transcends the emotional upheavals, the emotional "highs" and "lows." It's always there. It's the "you" that bubbles up from within and surrounds you with love and peace and makes you happy.

I dreamed that I was at the College of Metaphysics and Jonathan (one of the college students) was getting ready to transplant some cactus plants that had bloomed. I was astounded to see the cacti which had huge, beautiful pink flowers — the most gigantic flowers I'd ever seen on a cactus. I marvelled at Jonathan's ability to grow such lovely flowers and wanted to learn how.

This dream was the answer to a prayer. My husband had recently had a near-death experience which frightened me, bringing my attention to the gap between my belief that life exists beyond the physical and my own attachment to him being here in this physical body this lifetime. I had seen and heard accounts of people who had also had near death experiences, and their conclusion was that death was a wonderful, free, uplifting experience, moving into the light with perfect love and peace and no fear. Although I had had experiences like this in meditation and astral projection, I was still emotionally attached and therefore afraid when faced with death. I prayed, prior to my meditation, to know this reality and to be truly at peace with death.

After meditation, I went to bed and had this dream which was telling me there is a subconscious aspect of myself *(Jonathan)* which has produced much growth and understanding *(the flowers)* of the Self that is not physical. The *cactus* is a desert plant and the *desert* symbolizes the non-physical or inner consciousness. The dream reminded me of experiences I'd already had of being at home in the inner levels of consciousness; therefore, there was no need for me to fear. There was a need for me to bring this understanding more into my conscious awareness. *(I wanted to learn to grow the flowers.)*

How can we become connected with our soul and know, consciously, the Real Self? The simplest way to begin is to learn to remember and interpret our dreams. Every night when we sleep, we remove our attention from the conscious mind and physical senses. We are not aware of sounds, sights, smells, or tastes. We are not aware of bodily sensations. We are not aware of conscious thoughts. Yet, we still exist. Where do we go during this dream time?

We go within, to the inner levels of consciousness. This is the residence of the soul. Because the soul is the "Real Self" that is eternal, these experiences in the inner levels of consciousness oftentimes carry with them a mystical, numinous quality. Often, people wake up from a dream with the feeling that something very special and holy has occurred. And, in truth, it has! In our dreams we connect with Universal Truth. We experience the unlimited freedom of the Real Self. Although in our waking life we can become engrossed in physical limitations, in our dreams we experience the truth that we are in fact spiritual.

I was in a parking garage, trying to find my car, when I became aware I was being followed by someone sinister. I was afraid and tried to run from him when all of a sudden I realized I could fly. I took off and soared through the air, trying to find the way out of the garage. I kept coming up against walls, and then I thought to myself, "All I have to do is image the sky and I can go there." So I imaged the sky beyond the roof of the garage, and suddenly I was outside! I felt so free I thought I would burst! I thought, "up" and went up; thought "right" and went right. It was amazing that I could go anywhere I wanted and it was so easy.

This dream is an example of an out-of-body experience. All of us actually leave our physical body at night when we sleep. As in waking life, the only limitations that exist are in our own consciousness. When we think, "I can't," we can't! We put up walls by imagining everything that restricts us. In this dream I encountered the freedom of imagining where I wanted to go and using my will to do it. When I decided to soar beyond the walls that I thought were keeping me in, I could do it by deciding to raise my attention to the *sky* (superconscious awareness, or awareness of the spiritual Self). This freedom is very real, and a dream such as this gives us the experience of knowing how powerful the imagination and will can be. At the time I had this dream, I was unhappy with my job, feeling as if I "had to" go to work every day in activity that I found boring. I didn't really want to change jobs because I was making decent money and the hours I worked were very compatible with my needs at that time. But I didn't like spending so much time doing what seemed to me to be meaningless work (filing, typing, and other clerical duties). I felt trapped.

When I awoke from the dream, the experience of flying was so exhilarating and joyful, it stimulated me to want the same joy in my waking state! When I interpreted the dream it became clear to me that I was trapping myself in my own walls of limitation. I had chosen that job for convenience—it was a short drive to get to work and the hours and money were good. It was up to me to create a spiritual purpose for the work which would give it meaning. The job itself was not the problem, it was my attitude about it. This is what the dream was telling me: I needed to create a spiritual purpose and all it required was a change in my thinking to do so. I decided to use the job to learn service, to be a cheerful giver because, as it says in the Bible, "God loves a cheerful giver." Changing my attitude enabled me to be free once again, even in the same physical situation.

As children, many of us were told by well-meaning parents, "Don't worry, dear. It was just a dream. It wasn't real." Not true! Dreams are real. They are actual experiences in the inner levels of consciousness. The truth is that they are not physical. And so, simply by remembering a dream we experience ourselves as spiritual beings. No wonder it is such a nourishing experience to dream!

One way this knowledge can be of great benefit is for healing. A person's body becomes ill because their thinking is unhealthy, that is, out of alignment with Universal Law. Oftentimes, sick people become engrossed in their disease. Yet, in dreams, blind people can see, lame people can walk, asthmatics can breathe. Who is this Self that is whole and healthy? The Real Self, the soul. Remembering dreams can help a person who is ill recognize that their essence is not sick; it is whole and capable. Sometimes the experience of being whole in the dreamstate can stimulate a person to believe in their power to heal.

A terminally ill patient had the following dream:

I was discussing metaphysics with a little Oriental boy who wanted to show me metaphysical trinkets. These were little stones that had some special metaphysical significance. His mother didn't want him to have anything to do with me because she was afraid he might be hurt by being in contact with me since I was sick. The little boy recognized me and wasn't at all afraid. He wanted to give me the stones because he knew I was interested in his soul.

Then the scene changed and I was in a big city like Chicago, walking down the street. I saw an Asian man about 16 years old. He invited me up to his apartment and I noticed how neat and clean and organized his apartment was. I was impressed because he was living on his own. We made instant friends and talked about deep subjects in life. We'd eat healthy food and have tea and talk. The place had plants and flowers on the balcony and was full of oxygen.

Sometimes from the street I'd look up and see him meditating and reading. He was kind of unusual because at first glance it looked like his face was painted on, like a traditional Oriental appearance, but on closer look I could see all of his different expressions. Somewhere in the dream I realized that this young man was the same little boy from the earlier part of the dream, and in this second part of the dream I was not at all sick.

The man who had this dream reported that he awakened from it "feeling uplifted and connected again." It occurred shortly after an episode during which he was hospitalized — the third hospitalization in four months. Much of his life was consumed with fear, illness, hospitals, and medicine. Interpreting the dream revealed to him that by changing his thinking and using will power he could be released from the fear and be at peace.

The dreamer was Caucasian, and a *person of a different race* in a dream symbolizes an aspect that is foreign to your own way of thinking. The dreamer's familiar way of thinking was that of being sick and restricted by physical limitations. The foreign way of thinking, symbolized by the *little Oriental boy,* is the reality of metaphysics, life beyond the physical. The *boy's mother* (a subconscious aspect) didn't want the little boy to be in contact with the dreamer, showing that this unhealthy thinking is anathema to the subconscious which wants understanding. *Giving the stones* to the dreamer shows that giving and using the will *(stone)* are essential for caring for the soul. Later on in the dream when the young *Asian man is meditating,* it shows that this inner listening is also foreign to the dreamer but necessary for peace of mind.

This dream was showing the dreamer all of the inner resources he had to be whole: will power *(the stones),* inner listening *(meditation),* breath of life or spirit *(oxygen),* productive knowledge *(healthy food),* and an ordered mind *(the neat and clean apartment).* It was significant that the *Oriental boy* had these, showing that the dreamer had the potential but not the practice and use of them, since they are foreign to his way of thinking. *Face* in a dream symbolizes identity, and the dreamer's recognition that the face at first seemed painted on shows that he pretends to identify with the qualities the Oriental boy represents.

The dream seemed especially significant to the dreamer at the time he had it. He felt uplifted because in the dream state he experienced himself as whole and healthy. In his waking state, he was often depressed because his illness was a continual drain on his energy. He was having difficulty believing that he could ever be happy or healthy again and struggled to have any hope. Dreams come from the Self that is eternal and the dreamer got to taste the truth of eternal life, a taste of alignment with the spirit that is whole. It was a stimulus to him to make some changes and resurrect his consciousness.

Dreamers oftentimes wake up with a feeling that a dream is particularly profound, so dreams can nudge us to take action on ideas we may have thought about but have procrastinated acting upon:

I have a recurring dream that occurs at certain periods in my life; then I'll go for a long time and not have it. This is the dream: I go into this house that is very big and luxurious. It is beautiful and filled with antiques which are made of rich wood and are very valuable. I go through the rooms of the house and always find that there are more rooms, each one more beautiful than the next.

The woman who told me this dream said that she always felt wonderful after having it, but there was also a sense of melancholy (when she woke up) that she didn't have the dream all the time. A *house* symbolizes your mind and *furniture* symbolizes tools of the mind. I told her that the times she had this dream were times when she was exploring her mind and discovering that it is vast, full of resources, and contains tools of great value. When she heard the interpretation, the woman said, "I can't believe it! You must have a crystal ball; I always have this dream during the times in my life when I meditate. When I'm meditating it is very clear to me that there is so much more to my mind, so much for me to discover! When I stop meditating, the dream stops and I am always sad that I don't meditate as regularly as I'd like to."

This demonstrates a great benefit of knowing how to interpret dreams: it will show you patterns in your life that you can understand and change. After this woman had the dream interpreted she made a commitment to meditate every day, as she could see that the warm and wonderful feeling that the dream emanated was, in fact, an expression of the centering her daily meditation was producing in herself.

The following dream is another example of a spiritual experience that was a great stimulus even before the dreamer had it interpreted:

I walked up the stairs to my grandmother's attic and when I got there I saw my grandmother standing and smiling. She was glowing with a breathtakingly beautiful light. She was holding a jewelry box filled with jewelry. She smiled as she held it out to me and then gave me rings to put on four fingers of my right hand.

The young woman who had this dream told me she woke up with tears of joy in her eyes. The dream occurred during a spiritual festival known as Wesak, when the full moon is in Scorpio. It is important to be especially attentive during this time period, because Wesak dreams can give you insight into your soul's purpose and spiritual assignment in life. The *attic* symbolizes the superconscious mind or highest part of mind; the *grandmother* is a superconscious aspect. *Jewelry* is the value of the Self and *rings* symbolize commitment. *Light* is awareness.

This dreamer was being told that she had made a commitment to spiritual awareness and was ready to pursue a higher calling. She told me that she prayed daily to have her purpose in life revealed to her, because she believed that it was important to serve others and she wanted to live a Godly life. The dream was affirming her devotion.

People who remember their dreams radiate light. You can see it in their eyes and in their countenance, you can hear it in their voice. They are peaceful. They are connected with their inner source. Most children exhibit this radiant joy. Even when someone doesn't know how to interpret a dream, there is still a dawning recognition that the dream experience itself is profound and sacred. The next dream was the beginning of a new way of life for a young woman who was in-between adolescence and adulthood, trying to decide what to do with her life. The idea of living a purely physical existence, working and making money without any deeper purpose, left her "feeling as though my future was looking rather bleak. Then I had a dream:

In the dream I was standing at the top of the stairs on the outside of a white building gazing out over the most beautiful green landscape I had ever seen. The sun was brightly shining in a clear, blue sky. I saw many people engaged in activity together in the yard below. I could also see stacks of mattresses through a door at the top of the stairs. At one point we all gathered together for a meal. I felt such a strong sense of peace within and retained this feeling after I awoke and throughout the day. I never recorded this dream, but it did stick with me. It gave me a taste of peacefulness and love that I had never experienced before and I always wanted the dream to remain a part of me."

Her story continues, "When I was on lesson five in the first series of lessons in the School of Metaphysics, I was given the opportunity to visit the College of Metaphysics for the first time. We arrived at the college late at night so I was unable to see the campus clearly. We all spent the next day in the gorgeous sunshine beautifying the 'Dream Valley' house, a bed and breakfast located on campus in the breathtaking valley of the Niangua River. That afternoon we arrived back at the main building. As we turned onto the driveway up to the building, I was shocked and amazed at what I saw. I was suddenly reminded of a dream I had several months before. As I looked over the land I realized that those were the same hills and trees, the same house and clear blue, bright sky I had experienced in that dream. Although at first I did have some doubt, after I went into the chapel at the top of the stairs of this white main campus building and saw stacks of mattresses, it was confirmed. I really had dreamed about this place.

At that instance, I knew that I was where I was supposed to be and I then made the decision to be a College of Metaphysics student. I knew I had a future — a very bright future."

This is called a precognitive dream; "pre," meaning *before*, and "cognitive," meaning *knowing*. Because we dream in the subconscious mind or inner levels of consciousness, our dream experiences enable us to draw upon the power of the subconscious mind, which is intuition. The subconscious mind is not limited by time or space or distance. Our thoughts of today create our lives tomorrow, and the subconscious mind can therefore perceive how the energy of our thoughts is moving toward a probable future. Thus, this dream experience gave the young woman a preview of her future, and helped her confirm that she was choosing the right path for her education, happiness, and peace of mind.

All minds are joined in subconscious mind, so dreaming lets us know that we are linked with other people and with a greater reality. Sometimes the first "psychic" happenings people recognize are those which occur in dreams. Clairvoyance (clear seeing, or having visions), astral projection, and telepathy (mind-to-mind-communication) can all occur in dreams.

Many people report having dreams of loved ones who have died, showing that life exists beyond the physical body and physical senses and all of life is united in a great web. You know when a dream is an actual communication with another mind when there is no verbal communication, just telepathy, in the dream:

Shortly after my grandmother died, I went to bed and as I drifted off to sleep it felt like there was someone lying next to me, but no one was there. Then I smelled a wonderful rose perfume, like the one my grandmother always wore. I felt her stroking my hair and saw her smiling face. She didn't say anything but I was flooded with her love and I knew that she was with me.

The young woman who had this dream was very close to her grandmother and this dream helped her to be at peace with her grandmother's death. She believed that her grandmother would be okay and this dream left her with a great sense of comfort.

The dream experience itself is rewarding because our dreams connect us with our soul. The messages they reveal come from and concern the spiritual Self. When we turn away from our inner nature we become unhappy, distressed, or angry. When we align with our inner, spiritual Self, we know how to be fulfilled and live with joy. Dreaming gives us a taste of the deep peace that comes from being in contact with our inner Self, the Real Self. Whether through flying, foreseeing the future, linking our mind with an entity in the spirit world, or experiencing miraculous healing, dreams introduce us to our vast potential as spirit. Our nightly experiences show us that there is much more to us than meets the eye!

Every day we are faced with experiences for our learning, decisions to make, and actions to take. Knowing how to remember and use our dream time can make the difference between activities we "get through" or "get over with" and experiences that are meaningful and enriching. Interpreting our dreams helps to shed more "light" on the decisions we face. Dreams are always truthful because they come from the inner self which can only relate truth, so they can help us make choices that will be productive. They can be instrumental for developing security and peace of mind. Dreams are a wonderful tool for guidance and self awareness, to learn to align our conscious mind with the best interest of our soul and spirit.

Learning what our dreams are telling us about ourselves as a soul enables us to live a more purposeful existence, drawing forth our full potential. As we each become more aware of our own inner nature, we can give more to one another. Establishing connections with our own soul and among all souls awakens us to the truth that we are all of divine origin and are intricately linked in a harmonious whole. Dreaming lets us shine our light more brightly.

Dr. Laurel Clark has been teaching metaphysics since 1979 and is currently a faculty member of the College of Metaphysics. She is an ordained minister in the Interfaith Church of Metaphysics, a pastoral counselor, and intuitive reporter. She has served on the Board of Governors of SOM since 1982 and is also Senior Editor of Thresholds Quarterly.

Children's Dreams

by Dr. Pamela Blosser

Little Emma woke up suddenly, startled by a dream she had just had. A green monster had been chasing her. He had red eyes and sharp teeth. He had almost grabbed her with his big sharp claws. Emma peered into the dark, afraid that the monster might be lurking in the black recesses of her room or even hiding under her bed ready to grab her if she got up. Emma felt helpless and alone.

"Mommy! Mommy!" she cried out. Footsteps through the darkness brought growing comfort to little Emma.

"What is it, Emma? Did you have a bad dream?" Emma's mother held her and kissed her forehead. "You're okay, Emma. It was just a bad dream. You're safe and nothing's going to hurt you." She stroked Emma's hair until Emma had fallen asleep again.

How many times around the world do children call out for comfort in the night because their dreams have disturbed them? And how many times each night do parents tell their children it was just a dream? Just a dream. What does that mean, just a dream? It means it is not real and has little to no meaning. Yet to the child the dreams are real. They are exhilarating when they are flying. They are scary or so happy the child might laugh or cry out loud in their sleep.

not real in the sense that if you dreamed you were

you wouldn't be hurt as if you were in a car wreck

physical day-to-day experiences. Yet they are real happenings within the subconscious mind of each individual. They are real vibratory messages that relate the dreamer's conscious state of awareness coming from the inner mind to the outer mind during the sleep state. They are real perceptions within the conscious mind and brain of the dreamer. To discount dreams means you discount that you are a soul and that there is a link between the outer consciousness and the inner consciousness. Children still have an open channel to the subconscious mind, so they remember their dreams readily. It is important for parents and other adults to aid children by giving them a place to talk about their dreams as a real experience. Teaching children in this way insures that the connection to the subconscious mind will stay open during adolescence and into the adult years making the individual more grounded.

Because dreams relate the conscious state of awareness of the dreamer, parents can learn a lot about children by their dreams. What is going on inside the child's head is clearly related in dreams, so parents have a direct link to the inner thoughts and experiences of children through their dreams. It is of the utmost importance for teachers, and parents to be able to interpret their own dreams so they can teach children how to understand what their dreams are telling them. Dreams are a key to understanding self and more deeply understanding others.

When Linda was little her mother didn't know how to help her with her dreams. She wasn't satisfied when her mother told her to go back to sleep because it was just a dream. Linda sensed that there was some kind of meaning to her dreams. When she got old enough she began to research on her own to discover the meaning of her dreams. Linda now has four children of her own.

Every morning she asks them three questions about their dreams. *"Did you remember your dream? What was the dream about? Was the dream in color?"* She tells her children that if they have a problem in their waking life they can ask for an answer in their dreams. And if something in a dream disturbs them they can control it.

Linda has come to understand and know her children and know what they are going through as they have shared their dreams with her. One of her children, David, dreams about his teddy bear and its extended teddy bear family. She describes David as the most sensitive and maternal of her children. *Toys* in a dream symbolize how the imagination is being applied as ideas are developed and matured. David's dreams about the teddy bear and its relatives symbolize that he is learning how his own imaginative thoughts are related to each other, how one thought leads to another and what effect his ideas have on other people.

Her daughter, Cassandra, has a practical, down-to-earth approach to life. In her dreams she is a problem solver. Linda says that if their family is trying to find a solution to a question, like how to fix things around the house, Cassandra will tell her mother she had a dream about how to solve the problem. This is not only a result of Cassandra's way of thinking, but also a result of Linda's teaching that you can get answers to questions through dreams.

Linda says that her eldest son, even though in his waking life he is the most strong-willed, has the most nightmares of all her children. A nightmare is the subconscious mind's way of communicating to the conscious mind when there is something in life that is not understood and needs to be given attention. In the case of John Paul, when he was a baby, Linda herself was young and trying to figure out her life. Although these are John Paul's dreams, as an infant he was intimately linked with his mother on a mental level; therefore his mother's thoughts of insecurity and uncertainty had a profound influence on his developing mind. By the time she had the other children she was much more settled and sure of what she wanted. Yet John Paul's reaction to the issues that were a part of his mother's consciousness have not been resolved in his own mind.

Her eldest daughter, Stephanie, often dreams about flying in airplanes or swimming with dolphins. Experiences like these are out-of-body or astral projection experiences. It is not unusual for children to be aware of flying in their dreams. This is because children are still closely linked and identify with their subconscious mind or soul. The soul is not restricted to the physical body and can easily move through time and space. Therefore it's easy for children to leave their bodies during sleep and move through time and space. This motion is remembered when they wake as swimming or flying. Often they remember how free they felt as they flew when they woke up from such a dream.

Linda doesn't always know what the dream means but she says that by giving her children a place to talk about their dreams she knows it helps them. They know they can come and talk to her if they need to. They know she will listen to them, accept what they have to say and teach them what she knows.

Parents who learn how to interpret dreams open an expanded world for themselves and their children. They can help them solve problems. They can know when their child is troubled and what that trouble is related to. They can know what their child is thinking that the child might not be aware of himself or not want to talk about with the parents. They can know how their child responds to the world — do they roll with the punches or are they more sensitive to what is going on around them? How easy is it for them to change or adapt to the changing factors of their environment? Understanding children's dreams gives parents a more well-rounded view of their children. What they observe on the outside is complemented with what they learn about on the inside through their dreams.

When a soul enters the physical body it is immersed into thoughts, words, and actions. The outer conscious mind is like a sponge that absorbs this stimuli into the brain. The individual is still very much aware of itself as soul and the freedom the soul has outside the body. During the early years there may be dreams of flying or meeting angels and other heavenly beings. Four year old Iris talks about meeting her guardian angel in her dreams. She says she and her guardian angel fly together and sometimes she talks to Iris. This indicates Iris's awareness of herself as a soul and not just a physical being. Since our soul is closer to our true nature than our physical bodies, it is important to aid the child to keep this connection open and alive. Talking about dreams and learning about them is one way to do this, since the dream is coming from the soul or subconscious mind.

It is the child's urge to explore and gather information of a physical nature so the conscious mind and brain can function and reason. With each experience, links are made in the brain and stored to be used for the development of reasoning. When Hezekiah was four years old he had dreams related to what he was linking together in his life.

Franklin (his favorite stuffed animal, a turtle) fell into the pond. Pam and I were at the pond and a car came and ran over a basket of dinosaurs and they were pushed into the water.

Franklin is a toy and *toys* symbolize the use of imagination. *Water* is conscious life experiences. This means that Hezekiah is using his imagination in his everyday life. *Dinosaurs* are old creatures that are in fact extinct, symbolizing ancient pathways connected with the superconscious mind. There is an innate desire within us all to fulfill our potential. The superconscious mind holds within it a blueprint for fulfilling this spiritual potential, which is to create, to give, to learn and grow to a point of mastery. These urgings are ancient, buried deep within the heart, mind and soul of us all. Pam is one of Hezekiah's *teachers* which symbolizes a superconscious aspect. Children are stimulated by parents, teachers and other adults around them as to how they would want to be when they grow up. What parents and teachers symbolize in a dream are ideals we aspire to emulate. A *car* is the physical body. The dinosaurs are toys so this symbolizes how Hezekiah is using his imagination to link this urge of who he wants to become to physical life and experiences, maybe even what he would like to look like physically when he is older.

In another dream he told his mother:

We were in the kitchen. There was a lion and the lion had two baby lions and they were under the oven. I was holding Franklin and tigers came up to Franklin and me.

The *kitchen* is a place where food is prepared. *Food* symbolizes knowledge. In order to receive knowledge there must be desire to know and a curiosity — a question in the mind reaching for an answer. This is the state of mind a *kitchen* symbolizes in a dream. The *lions* and *tigers* are *animals* which represent brain pathways. *Franklin* represents the use of imagination.

Learning and growth means new ideas are presented to us that we try out in our life. As children we experiment with the ideas through the act of playing, singing, drawing, acting, and so on. If these ideas bring us some kind of benefit we continue doing them until they are a part of our outward identity. "This is the way I am" we might tell others because we respond in this manner without giving it a second thought. This is a brain pathway. Hezekiah's dream is revealing this learning process. Hezekiah spends much time playing at being fierce, brave and strong. This is what the lions and tigers represent.

When Hezekiah was five he had another dream about tigers. Hezekiah was in a car where there were tall buildings.

There was a tiger. The tiger was jumping off buildings and roaring and stuff like that. It was the Exotic Animal Paradise, even worse than the Exotic Animal Paradise. The tiger wasn't in a cage, so me and mommy drove away from there. Mommy was driving. We went into a big box to hide.

The Exotic Animal Paradise is a park where animals roam uncaged and people drive through in their cars to view them. The reason he said it was worse than the Exotic Animal Paradise was that in his dream the cats were roaming uncaged, and at the theme park the wild cats are caged. Again as in the previous dream, Hezekiah is forming a pathway of strength and courage. However in this dream it is one he doesn't feel he has control of. His mother told me he had this dream about the time his father was gone for several days to visit his ailing father. This was the first time Hezekiah and his father had been separated.

The varied experiences in a child's life are what fill the brain with information. Some of the experiences they may understand and feel in control of and some they may not. Because the reasoning ability is developing children may not always be able to draw an accurate conclusion from the experiences they have. When there is an incident that they don't understand, don't feel they can control, or that scares them in their waking life, this reaction will show up in their dreams as monsters or animals that scare them — bears, lions, gorillas — as in Hezekiah's dream of the uncaged tigers.

When Greg was four years old he dreamed of a threatening looking lady who resembled the licorice character in the Candyland game coming through the window into his room. Greg's bedroom was next to the garage, and in his waking life he feared that someone might be able to come into his room through the garage. Because Greg experienced fear about someone coming through the window in his bedroom, the bedroom became a perfect symbol for a deeper fear that the dream was describing. A *bedroom* symbolizes a place in the mind for assimilating what is being learned from the experiences of life. The *threatening lady* represents a thought that is threatening Greg's sense of security and safety. The dream signifies that Greg's own imagined fears were interfering with his ability to learn from the experiences around him. His mother mentioned how Greg seemed to be sensitive and afraid at times.

Three year old Adam had a recurring dream that the Incredible Hulk was after him. He would wake up crying. The *monster* signified there was a part of himself, such as a way of thinking that he didn't understand, felt threatened by, and had no control over. His mother and father had divorced. Adam's family had been destroyed, threatening his own sense of security. He didn't know how to reconstruct his family or control his environment as he witnessed his sense of security dissolving. And he was afraid of what might happen now that his family no longer existed.

If a fear is not understood, each time there is an experience similar to the original one, the individual will unconsciously react as if it were the original experience. The subconscious mind will relay a message to the conscious mind that the same reaction is being triggered again. This message will come in the form of a recurring dream. For example, Adam's fear continued each time he imagined he might lose something he loved that brought him security.

Let's say his grandmother, to whom he was quite attached, became ill and he began to imagine she was going to die. His subconscious mind would relay a message that he was experiencing the same type of insecurity he experienced when his parents divorced. The message would come in the form of the same Incredible Hulk dream.

Recurring nightmares especially from childhood are the subconscious mind's way of letting the dreamer know there is still unfinished business from childhood or the past that is cropping up again and needs to be addressed. Jeff had disturbing dreams about monsters when he was a child and to this day still dreams about them periodically. This is telling Jeff that there are unconscious reactions related to unresolved issues from the past.

Children want to have a sense of control in their lives as they are growing up to be more independent beings and also because much of their life is influenced by other people's decisions. Sometimes children feel like they are not in control of their lives. When this idea becomes an issue for them it will appear in a dream. Beverly felt out of control of her life which manifested in a recurring dream:

Baby aspirin were stacked up around me in my bed and then slowly fell over on top of me.

A *bed* symbolizes a place in mind for assimilation or how we learn from our day-to-day experiences. *Aspirin* symbolizes a dependency on something outside yourself for your state of well-being and therefore the need to exercise the will power. The action of the aspirin falling in around her represents feeling closed in. The dream means that as she was learning from her everyday experiences she felt closed in by her dependency on an outside influence that brought her a sense of well-being.

About the time Beverly was having this recurring dream her parents were going through a divorce. This was a time when divorce was not as prevalent as it is today. Beverly felt isolated from others, wanted someone to give her comfort and, because it was not forthcoming, experienced self-pity. The self-pity was represented in the dream by the *baby aspirin*. She wanted something to make everything better. Her self-pity was closing in on her consciousness and distracting her from the learning being offered in the situation at hand, to become more self-reliant and independent.

As dreams reveal when children or adolescents are having difficulty as they mature, they will also reveal when they are reasoning and responding productively to the situations around them. For example, here is Allison's dream:

I was lost at the airport and separated from my parents. Angela Lansbury from the T.V. show "Murder She Wrote" found me and solved the mystery to locate my parents.

Because *airports* are places involving planes, cars, buses and lots of people, they represent how you express Self individually and in groups. *Angela Lansbury* is a female, the same sex as Allison, the dreamer. That means she is an aspect, a quality or personality trait, of Allison's conscious or outer mind. *Parents* represent aspects of the Superconscious Mind. As mentioned in Hezekiah's dream, this is a part of the Self that holds the plan for the fulfillment of your potential. Great wisdom and guidance comes from the Superconscious Mind. Allison's dream means that as she expresses Self to others (*airport*) she is using an aspect of her Conscious Mind to be in touch with this deepest part of her inner Self that offers guidance and wisdom.

Here is a recurring dream that Allison had between the ages of eight and ten.

I was being kidnapped by people I didn't know who had Mohawk haircuts. They took me to a huge indoor playground with tubes, mazes, nets, slides and ball pits. It turned out to be a lot of fun.

People who you don't know represent qualities in yourself that you are unconscious of. *Hair* represents conscious thoughts. *Being kidnapped* represents experiencing being out of control. The *playground* represents use of the imagination. In this dream when Allison begins thinking in ways where she feels out of control (*being kidnapped by people with Mohawk haircuts*), and she uses her imagination (*the playground*), she can figure out what to do and things turn out for her. Allison is usually a positive person, creative, and imaginative. These dreams illustrate these traits in her.

Adolescence is a time of making strides toward personal independence and empowerment. It is a time when physical maturation is quickened. Hormones are starting to be active which means the creative energy or kundalini is being awakened. This is the time when children begin thinking seriously about what they want to do with the adult years of their lives and who they want to be. Whatever they have been imagining adulthood to be, they are now starting to bring that into a reality in their life. There are major changes physically, emotionally and mentally that can sometimes shake their world. The following dream of ten year old Bea reflects this state of consciousness.

I had a mom and a dad, but it was not my real mom and dad and we lived in a three story house and we heard news about a tyrannosaurus and velociraptor in town. Me and my family were driving to the store and we felt the vibration of the dinosaurs' feet and we drove back home and hid. The dinosaurs came and roared and chased after us and I woke up.

There are many indications of changes occurring in Bea's life from the dream. First she was with parents who weren't her own in her waking state. *Parents* represent aspects of the

Superconscious Mind. Since these weren't her real parents and she doesn't know them, this shows Bea is moving into new, unfamiliar areas of spiritual unfoldment, wisdom and guidance. *House* represents the mind. The fact that it is three stories indicates the awareness of the conscious, subconscious and superconscious minds — the physical, soul and spirit. As mentioned before *dinosaurs* symbolize ancient spiritual compulsions connected with how we fulfill our potential to create, give, learn and grow to a point of mastery.

Bea's dream symbolizes that there are awarenesses of how she can create that are overwhelming to her. Adolescents are at a threshold of their life where many changes internally and externally are occurring. Often they begin to entertain the thought that they could do something that would change the world. Their minds are free to imagine what they would like to do with their life and how they will make a difference to those around them.

At the same time what they have seen in the adults around them is the reality of the possibility for their life. If the adults are alive and learning, if they love the work they do, if they are passionate about certain causes in life, or have interesting and creative hobbies, if spiritual devotion is alive and important to them, then the child will reach for adulthood. If the adults are bored, have little purpose in their lives, if they live from day to day and dislike the work they do, then this gives the child little to aspire to. Most children have had a combination of both types of experiences and therefore have a range of thoughts and feelings about growing up.

The universal condition existing in our society, one that views life from a materialistic, humanistic point, brings about a deeper, more subtle dilemma, often unconscious to the individual. In American culture, we are rooted in physical experience and materialism. Collectively our culture has agreed that we are strictly physical beings having physical experiences with an occasional spiritual experience. Children are a different case. It's okay for them to be free, spontaneous, have imaginary playmates and fly in their dreams. What this means is that it's okay for them to still be in touch with themselves as a soul having physical experiences for the sake of learning and evolution.

At some point in puberty the individual knows that the consciousness must change in order to "grow up" and be accepted as an adult by others. They must accept the image of adulthood they have been shown in earlier years and be like what they perceive society has deemed adults ought to be.   Instead of awakening, the process of growing up is seen as a sense of loss. It means a shutting down of creativity right when the creative energy, the kundalini, is beginning to be experienced more profoundly. This energy should be used to imagine what they want to do with their adult life and how wonderful this process is. Instead of awakening and understanding this awakening, it is only seen as becoming sexually active. As one matures and accepts adulthood and its physical trappings, if one is thinking materialistically the doorway between the soul and the outer self is closed off. This is a time of grieving and is often experienced as depression, anger or a general feeling that life just isn't going right. I have talked to several of my adult friends who remember that the seventh or eighth grade was the worst year of their life. These attitudes manifest in a variety of types of dreams.

Jennifer, a senior in high school, dreamed she was tied up to a chair and forced to watch as her mother was killed. This dream upset her so much that she came home early from school the next day. Not only were the dream images disturbing but they also reflected a deeper thought that was equally disturbing. Being *tied to a chair* symbolizes a sense of restriction. Being *forced* means the dreamer doesn't feel she has control over the experience.

Jennifer's mother in the dream symbolizes an aspect of the Superconscious Mind, the highest part of the mind that is closest to one's divine nature and holds the potential for unfoldment. *Death or killing* in a dream means change. Jennifer's mother *being killed* in the dream means Jennifer's perception is changing of what her true nature is. This could be the killing of her own sense of herself as a spiritual being. She has no choice in the matter. It is out of her control.

Susan, a teenager, had recurring dreams of betrayal. One specific scenario was that one of her girlfriends was coming between her and her boyfriend and they were breaking up as a result. In dream symbols *a person of the opposite sex* is an aspect of the inner or subconscious mind. This is an aspect of soul. The *other female* is an aspect of Susan's conscious or outer mind. The action of breaking up represents the separating or closing off of the conscious and subconscious minds. What Susan's dream means is that an outer part of her conscious mind is usurping her ability to be connected to this familiar aspect of the subconscious mind. The joyous affiliation with her inner mind was no longer available to use and she feels betrayed.

When Alexis was 12 and 13 she had recurring dreams that she was falling into a black hole. She would wake up trying to catch her breath. *Earth* in a dream represents the inner mind substance that is available for creating. Adolescence is a time for creating many changes in your life. It can also be intimidating and overwhelming when the individual may not know what they want. In Alexis' case the dream was indicating that she needed to become more aware of what her desires were and how she thought. As she was changing she was losing a sense of who she was and what she wanted in life. Growing up is a time to build a more mature identity, one that we can reach for as our bodies mature into young men and women.

During her adolescence Debbie had a recurring dream. She would fall down in the hallway of her school and couldn't move her legs to get up. A *school* represents a place of learning in your mind and experiences. *Legs* represent forward motion. Debbie's dream symbolized that she felt helpless at times in being able to move forward in her learning. There were several years when Debbie was going to middle school that she had trouble with some of her subjects at school. New math was being introduced and she didn't understand the concepts. Her parents tried to help her but they didn't understand it either. There were obviously other areas where Debbie felt stifled in her learning whether it was her academic studies or of a personal nature. Debbie said the dream stopped after she got in college. Her grades had improved by that time, she had chosen her major and knew the career she wanted to pursue.

And then there are dreams of growing harmony within the mind and distancing the consciousness from that which is purely materialistic and physical in nature. Twelve-year-old Briana is striving to mature in a wholistic manner. Her life is surrounded by individuals who want to grow spiritually and are teaching her. She lives at the headquarters of the School of Metaphysics and is schooled by her parents as well as the teachers there. All disciplines are connected in her curriculum. When she cooks, for example, she also learns math, science, art, visualization, and service. Her dreams reflect how her spirituality is growing.

There was a stage in a theater. Linda, my mom, and a man I didn't know were all singing while the man played the electronic guitar with a puppet too. All of the girls also danced in ballet costumes. We all had silver diamonds on our foreheads because they would cover for the green diamonds for the main performance until we found the green ones.

When we all went backstage, Linda found some green duct tape to use for the green diamonds instead, even though my mom and I were looking for the green diamonds before Linda.

Theater represents an imaginative state of mind and the *stage* is the place of focus for the imagination. Briana's *mom* represents an aspect of superconscious mind; *Linda* represents an aspect of the conscious mind, and the *girls* are other aspects of the conscious mind. The *unidentified man* represents an aspect of the subconscious mind that Briana is not yet familiar with. *Singing* and *dancing* symbolize mental harmony; and *diamonds* are value. The diamonds were placed on their foreheads symbolizing value being placed on mental perception. *Duct tape* is used for joining or sticking objects together, so it represents a way to join or connect thoughts.

Briana's dream is telling her that she is imagining how harmony can exist among all parts of her mind and how valuable mental perception is. She is seeking to change how she values her perception. Until she finds this value she has a sense of value as well as a way to connect her perceptions. At a time in our society when for most people, the inner mind is shutting off from the outer mind, Briana is expanding her consciousness. She knows that mental perception is valuable and is valuing how she can keep the inner and outer selves connected. She is keeping the doorway between her conscious and subconscious minds open.

Dreams are a valuable tool for keeping this doorway open. One of the major functions of the subconscious mind is to receive the learning that has occurred in the conscious mind and to store it as wisdom or understanding. This assimilation process goes on while we are asleep. During our sleep time the subconscious mind reviews the learning for the past day and relates honestly where we are with our learning. Dream activity begins in the subconscious mind during this evaluation and assimilation process. Since the subconscious mind only knows learning, it will always relate truth. To understand your dreams and the dreams of your children means you have an honest appraisal of your or your child's conscious state of awareness. Dreams offer an avenue for the direct grasp of truth that lies in the subconscious mind. The subconscious mind always offers truth and learning to the dreamer. Understanding dreams means the individual's consciousness is reaching for truth and learning and this in turn harmonizes the activity of the outer mind to the inner, subconscious mind bringing the individual closer to Intuition.

Parents are wise to encourage their children to remember their dreams and to endeavor to understand what they mean. You can start talking about dreams with your children at any time and at any age. Everyone loves to talk about the dreams they've had and wants to know what they mean. Children are no exception. A dream notebook by the bed helps to have a place to write dreams down. Then bring the dream notebook to the breakfast table. For busy families who might not have time during the morning of a weekday, plan to talk about dreams on a weekend morning. If parents start asking their children what dreams they remembered, they will volunteer the dreams they've had.

Dreams reveal how you are learning and changing. It is a direct link to your soul, to your heart's desires and to your deep-seated fears. Dreams reveal so much about the individual that parents can learn a lot about their children from their dreams. Encourage your children to write down their dreams. Talk about the dreams with your children. And learn what the dreams are revealing so you can guide your child to a sense of peace and security and quicken their evolution. Being interested in your child's dreams in the least and knowing how to interpret them at best could be one of the most valuable gifts you could ever give your child.

Dr. Pamela Blosser has taught children and young people in various capacities throughout her adult life. She has taught in Montessori schools and studied, taught and directed at Schools of Metaphysics throughout the Midwest. A teacher in the School of Metaphysics since 1977, Dr. Pam serves in many capacities including instructor of metaphysics, minister at PeaceMakers gatherings each Sunday and director of Camp Niangua, the summer camp for young people.

Dreams and American Youth

by Damian Nordmann

The consciousness and decisions of the parents and all adults in our country have a huge impact on the consciousness of American youth. What the parents, adults, and elders decide to make right or to ignore molds and shapes the way children think and how they live. My parents divorced when I was fourteen years old. While this did not have a terribly detrimental effect on me, the attitudes and compulsive ways of thinking that each of my parents had did set the ground work for what became my attitude about life and what I would do or refuse to do to create and be happy. I always had some awareness of this, and I became very aware and clear as to how my thinking had been influenced when I started studying metaphysics, in particular dream interpretation.

I was eighteen when I met Oliver Seger, the director of the School of Metaphysics in Louisville, KY. He had given a lecture on dream interpretation at my high school humanities class one day. Unfortunately I missed that day of school, one of maybe four or five days that I missed during my Senior year. Everyone was telling me how they had their dreams interpreted and this meant that and what meant what in dreams. Phooey! No one could tell me what my dreams meant but me. I had known that for a long time. I had always remembered many of my dreams and often times I was quite sure what they were conveying to me. I certainly didn't need someone else telling me what my dreams were saying to me. I wasn't too disappointed that I had lost out on our special guest, I just kept doing the usual high school stuff. You know, homework, special assignments, projects, my church youth group, and of course hanging out with friends. My opportunity to learn about my dreams would come later.

It was the middle of November and my humanities teacher was taking us to his farm for his annual two days of outdoor education. This was optional, of course, for anyone not going could stay with a teacher of their choice to do homework and busy work, yeah right. I had missed the opportunity the previous year when I was in Mr. Holden's Junior English class and I had to listen to all the tales of fun, learning, and mayhem that went on. I was not about to let the chance get away from me again that year.

It was during the first night we were there that three men from the School of Metaphysics drove up. People were telling me that one of the men, Oliver, was the person who gave a presentation on dream interpretation. While we were still eating Oliver came over to my group of friends and sat with us. He said we all looked like a cozy tribe and a few of us laughed. I asked him if he knew anything about astral projection which was something I had gained an interest in during the last seven months. I thought he would shrug and say he knew a little bit of information on the topic. Instead he quickly replied with authority, "Astral projection is the process of consciously moving your attention away from your physical body and into the inner levels of mind." I was amazed that anyone in Louisville actually knew something about astral projection, let alone have some authority on the subject. I was really wanting to tell him of my friend's experience of being able to leave her body, but I wasn't sure how to respond to his quick answer to my question, so I listened.

Later on Oliver talked to the whole group about meditation. He talked about aligning the conscious and subconscious minds and attuning them to the superconscious mind, which he said was everyone's connection with God. I considered myself a very spiritual and religious person at that time, and I wasn't sure if I believed what he was saying, or not. It did strike a chord with me, though, because he had such authority and what he talked about could give me more power, which was what I was seeking at the time. Oliver told us about the sound of the Aum and we all chanted the Aum and meditated. During the chant there were a few people giggling a distance away from me, however my friends and the people near me were all quite serious about trying out this chant. The vibration and the feeling it created was intense. When we were finished I wanted to try it again, but I didn't want to look stupid for getting a bunch of people together to Aum loudly.

Even though I still wasn't so sure I bought into the dream interpretation, I wanted to learn meditation, and I was curious to see if the School of Metaphysics could teach me astral projection. I wrote a letter to the School of Metaphysics expressing my interest in their classes. My letter was answered, but I put off going to the classes for some time. A month and a half rolled by then I received a call from Oliver about a class starting. I said I would try to be there, but again I didn't make it. Oliver called me the next week and asked me if I wanted to be in the class. I said yes and he said I would need to come a half an hour early to catch up on what I had missed the previous week.

During the next several weeks and months a whole new way of thinking started to unfold for me. Much of it came from having my teacher, Oliver, interpret my dreams for me as I began to learn to interpret them for myself. It was after about the second or third week of class that I realized there was something to this dream interpretation. I had learned that my dreams were about me and my conscious state of awareness. I learned that we all dream in the Universal Language of Mind, which is a picture language. I learned some of the symbols such as animals represent habits or compulsions and that a car represents my physical body. What kept getting to me was how every week my teacher was able to tell me things about me that I had not told him. He could tell from my dreams if I had been undisciplined with my spiritual practices or if I had been thinking up some new idea. I was surprised and I wanted to know how he was doing it.

I was enjoying learning how to improve my concentration and understand the nightly messages given to me, then came the big dream. I awoke from it in the middle of the night and sat up straight in bed...

I'm just hanging out by the seaside with friends, and people from school. I climb down a cliff to some people playing a game in an out jutting no bigger than 5 X 5 square. I get frightened and stuck, but the two people down there a male and female my age say they will stay with me. Shortly thereafter I say I'll climb down because it's no big deal, but they find a way to make it even easier to help me.

I see people swinging as I sort of did to get up the cliff. People help each other. When I reach the top of the cliff overhanging the sea I notice there is a change. The air, the attitude has shifted. Someone new is there, a former friend of mine Matt Weckman. But he looks different. He's wearing a light blue sweater and jeans and his clothes look cleaner and nicer than usual. His hair is also short which is different than he is in physical life. He seems to be acting the same, but creepier. I go to talk to him, yet he seems to blow me off, ignoring my genuine concern for him. He goes and talks to my friend Natalie. Many of my friends are around. I wander off by myself then Matt issues some sort of challenge. As I'm striding from the edge of the cliff to another place I cut my finger deeply, but with minimal blood. I see a huge deep chunk of flesh is now missing, and I wonder why there is no pain. Re-approaching the cliff I look for Weckman and I notice the sea, the sun, and many sailing ships great and small coming and going. Weckman has left and Natalie has gone with him.

The next thing I know, my friends and I are in a house. We get a call from Natalie. Natalie wants someone to pick her up at Matt's way down on Taylor Blvd. I hear Matt yelling as if drunken and aggressive. He swears that we won't make it and that we're doomed. From out of the phone his voice shouts at my friends calling out his hatred of them. To Cali he says that she's a precious rich girl and something about the two of them living on different sides of town and her wealth and his poverty. I don't recall the others, and then I yank the phone cord out of the wall. I turn to a mirror and give a Kenpo salute. I say, "It has begun. We must now do what we must."

Demons, hallucinations, and spirits immediately begin taunting us. I tell my friends not to be afraid and that they are only mind games. Cali and Rush are near and I forget who else. The taunts are brutal voices telling us how we will die, and terrible pain and suffering. I don't believe a bit of it, even when the apparitions appear to me as people I know. We strike out to get Natalie, but my friends are forced to abandon me. I don't feel lonely though.

It's night and I am running along the streets with great speed, knowing that I can do anything with my mind, even change myself into a car, but that would be too easy. I must look like a car, because at first no one notices, and I use my will power to change the stoplights before I reach them. Some cars come up behind me and I'm forced to be me so I step onto the sidewalk as I see their headlights go by. I jump up onto the storefront out juttings and canopies because the demons are getting stronger. Two vampires appear one is Susan, the other is some other Oriental girl that I know from school. They tell me that I will die and that I will fail. They are bleeding and I feel for them. I tell them I will return.

I finally come up on the house quickly. It's not really Matt's house, but it could be. The demons and spirits are strongest here. I cry out, "In the name of God be gone! In the name of God be gone! In the name of God be gone!" Nothing harms me. As I enter I see Natalie and she gets behind me. Matt approaches about to attack, but I say the true name of Jesus, "In the name of Yahushua be gone!" four or five times. Each time it sends waves of pain into him. He looks different again. He's got bigger muscles then before, much more, and evil. He has people digging things up in his smelly, musty, broken down house, but they stay away. The men look fairly normal, Matt doesn't. I count 12 men before I turn to leave. As Natalie and I exit, Matt stands and swears he will not be beaten, he swears he'll destroy us. My friends are out on the street. I tell them that this is only the beginning, but we will succeed.

I didn't know if I should be shocked or amazed. The dream was one of the most real and vivid dreams I had ever had. I knew the dream had to have some very important meaning so I wrote it down immediately. Afterwards I noticed it was after three o'clock in the morning.

I found out later that the dream was about how I was motivating my Self and how the way I viewed my life was changing. *Matt* represented an aggressive conscious aspect of me that sometimes would get out of control. I had learned from my father to let things build up inside me until I was very angry or frustrated and then to dump everything out in an explosion of emotion. Each of my *friends* represented different aspects of me.

Natalie represented an inner aspect of magnetism and attraction. In the dream I rescued this aspect from my more sporadic quality. There were many other symbols in the dream and I learned what each one of them meant. The *cliffs* represented a challenge that was before me. The *vampires* and *demons* represented negative or unproductive aspects of me that needed to be changed or healed. My ability to run very fast was showing me how I was starting to learn to create much greater forward motion in my life. My ability to change the stop lights and jump high indicated an awareness in the power to use my mind to cause what I wanted. Matt wanting to kill me represented my need to change. *Death* in a dream represents change. The approach of both of my parents was usually to wait until things got bad before they would change. I adopted this attitude in many areas of my life. I wasn't sure yet how to cause changes to occur in my life so it all seemed very brutal and somewhat scary like in the dream.

After I had this dream I became much more determined to write down and interpret each of my dreams that I remembered. Each morning was exciting for me as I looked for something new to learn from my previous night's journeys. Every dream is about the dreamer. Dreams relate to us our conscious state of awareness. The dreams will always present truth, and they are showing what we were thinking and learning the day before we have them. This became more evident to me as I started to make connections between the interpretation of my dreams with what I knew I had actually done the day before. It became very important for me to pay attention and remember what I was thinking and feeling from the previous day. Sometimes I immediately knew what the dream was offering me, even before I wrote it down.

I was so excited about this new skill that I was developing, I started interpreting dreams for everyone I knew. I would spend my lunch period at school interpreting dreams for people I ate with. I would interpret the dreams of my friends in my youth group and friends that went to other high schools. I would even interpret the dreams of my family members when they would ask me to.

A couple of months after I started learning to interpret my dreams, I became acutely aware of how scattered and out of focus I often was. I had a dream that gave me much insight into this.

I'm at school. I see Laura and I give her a hug, but she gets mad because she thinks the hug is superficial and I don't care about her. I promptly give her another one and tell her not to worry. Later school lets out and I'm in a mad rush. Mr. Davis all of a sudden assigns a bunch of homework out of the blue. I'm scrambling to get my stuff together because I am afraid I will miss the bus. At one point many of my books and my binders are scattered on the floor so I have to waste even more time picking them up. I run down the stairs only to see that it is dark and rainy outside. The buses are already pulling away and leaving me behind. I yell and run after them, trying to find mine. Mine is gone and most of the rest leave. I see Rebecca Sherman merely standing outside. I go up and ask her if one of her parents will take me home. She suggests that we take one of the buses that is still running and unattended. We jump in and the front seat is like that of a truck's. She drives the bus and I notice how attractive she is looking. She is wearing a nice outfit, white or pink with a short skirt and lacy stockings. I put my hand on her leg and try to get close to her. She doesn't seem to mind so I get closer. She points out several other buses going to a compound nearby. I ask her a question about something. She refers my question to a University of Louisville watch I have on my wrist and something to do with Speed School.

Being in *school* indicates an attitude of learning. This is very important because life is a continual learning process. When we stop learning we stop creating, then we start to deteriorate mentally and physically. In this dream I was scrambling and hurrying. I wasn't prepared for the assignment that one of my teachers gave me. The hurrying in the dream showed me how hurried I was in my daily, conscious thinking. If you notice the more you try to hurry at something, the more mistakes you make and the longer it takes to do anything. This is how I was at that time. I could see how I had learned this from my parents as well. They were often procrastinating and then would try to accomplish a task in a rushed often scattered manner.

Mr. Davis, my Calculus teacher, represented an aspect of my Superconscious Mind. Superconscious Mind is the division of mind that we all have that connects us with all of creation. Within Superconscious Mind is our plan for being compatible with God and learning to be creators with God. In the dream Mr. Davis assigns homework that I am not prepared for which shows how I was not prepared mentally for responding to my own inner urge that comes from my superconscious Self. When I go outside in the dream the *sky* is dark which indicates how I was ignoring something in my conscious state of awareness.

The *school bus* represented an organization that was moving me towards learning. At the time I thought this was probably my high school youth group or the School of Metaphysics. Me running represented my desire and attempt to keep up with the organization and the learning it provided. *Laura* and *Rebecca* are both female which represents subconscious or inner aspects of me. There was affection for and an attempt to harmonize with these aspects of my Self. *Rebecca* represented an aspect of excellence and high standards. Because she was driving the bus this represented how I was using this aspect to help me get to where I was going. However, because I was not driving the bus, this showed how I needed to take more conscious control of where I was going with my life.

All of this made sense to me at the time. I was often putting off projects or goals then I would try to complete them in a hurried and inefficient manner. I was trying to gain the most I could from my high school, church youth group, and from the School of Metaphysics, but I never seemed to be able to keep up with all the ideas that were being presented.

Unfortunately, oftentimes the youth of our country are not sure what to think, what the difference is between right and wrong, or how to learn. With television, movies, magazines, and all manner of other stimuli and outside influences, children and adolescents can develop some rather bizarre ways of thinking. This dream showed me how my own thinking was somewhat backwards:

I find myself in my car with a thin, tall, straight-dark-haired man with brown eyes. He seems fairly nice if not a little weird. He keeps talking and talking. His demeanor gradually shifts from one of frightened kindness to psycho perversion. He mentions that he called my house. He asks me to take him home because he lives on Hurstbourne Lane. He even offers some money. When we get to a gas station he gets really weird. He takes some dollar bills off my dash board and says, "This is compensation." I tell him to give it back immediately and he does. He also has one of my mom's blank checks. I make him return that as well, but I lose all trust in the man. I tell him to give me gas money so he brings out two huge handfuls of quarters. He tells me to take them but that he'll burn down my house if I do. He tries to do something to me so I punch him three times. I'm not sure if I make him get out then or not, but he makes references to the fact that he knows where I live. That is all I can remember.

The main symbols in the dream were the *unfamiliar man*, my *car*, *gasoline*, and *money*. I did not know the *man* so he represented an unknown conscious aspect of me. My *car* represents my physical body. *Gasoline* represents energy, and *money* represents value. This dream was showing me how I didn't know how to use value or respect it. This is something my parents tried to teach me, yet they were not disciplined enough themselves to make sure I followed through on my commitments. Had they taught me early on the joy and value of working and accomplishment, then I think this dream would have been different, or would not have come up at all.

There is also an attitude of taking and stealing represented by the man trying to take my money and get a free ride home. There was conflict and distrust with this aspect of me which indicated how I distrusted and had conflict occurring within my Self during the day. Mistrust was the attitude I had as presented to me in my first intuitive health analysis I received from the School of Metaphysics. It was true that I had very little trust in my Self because I rarely followed through to completion on the many ideas and desires I had. This all made sense because I had been refusing to get a job and earn my own money. My parents also had a hard time getting me to follow through on things I said I would do so my overall sense of value and trust in my own ability to create was very low. After this dream and some related dreams I began to take greater actions to get a job I liked and looked for ways I could be of assistance to others.

Since those first months in the School of Metaphysics I have used my dreams for many wonderful transformations. I have come a long way from believing that no one could tell me what my dreams meant to now being a teacher who interprets other people's dreams, helps them to understand their meaning, and shows how they can be applied to their daily life.

I have a great respect for what my parents taught me and an acceptance in knowing they did the best with what they had. By using my dreams to understand my waking consciousness I have the opportunity to learn what my parents did not teach me. I envision a time when all parents learn dream interpretation for themselves and perhaps more importantly for their children. When parents value the messages of their own dreams they will see how desperately each soul that is in a young body wants to learn and to reach their full potential. Fears will be dispelled. Strengths will be recognized and fostered. Dream interpretation is the simplest and most accessible tool anyone has for understanding themselves. As adults and parents teach this to the youth we will see a generation of leaders and world servers come about, and we will have taken a giant leap towards peace for the whole planet.

Damian Nordmann is the Director of the School of Metaphysics in Oklahoma City. A high school student when he began his SOM studies, Damian is a graduate of the College of Metaphysics and has taught in Louisville, KY and Springfield, MO.

From Darkness to the *Light*

by Terry Martin

A soul incarns into a physical form to learn how to become like its Creator. Much of the early learning involves becoming familiar with the physical world. This includes learning how to move the body, receive through the senses and gradually incorporate information into the brain which will serve as the foundation throughout life.

From the perspective of a newborn child, the physical world is alien. The soul, having just incarned into an immature physical body, must become familiar with the workings of that body. Information is received through sensory input. The sense of touch is one of the first experiences a baby will have. Usually finding the gentle touch of a parent to be calming, the baby receives this information and stores it in the brain. The brain is like a brand new computer having no information until operating software has been installed. The brain awaits "input" and this occurs through the senses.

Newborn babies must learn of the physical world they have just entered. They have to learn to wield their physical body, learning to focus the eyes, exploring their world through the sense of touch and taste. They learn to identify vibrations through the touch of a gentle hand, the sound of music, the sight of stimulating color and the taste of nourishing foods.

A newborn has little to relate the new information to and has a great deal to learn about the physical world. Adults who observe a baby's expression and sense of wonder have a greater sense of appreciation about the physical world, viewing the world from the child's perspective. Often adults talk to babies in "baby talk" as if somehow they would be able to communicate with the child better by sounding like the baby as he or she is learning to understand words.

It is a misconception that babies cannot understand. Their connection with the subconscious mind transcends any physical limitation of language or experience and they are able to perceive the pictures that adults have within their minds.

I remember an experience with my nephew shortly around the age of six months. Brandon was not yet talking but he was very alert and attentive to what went on around him. My brother-in-law told a joke, as he is prone to do at family gatherings, and everyone laughed. Brandon joined in the laughter nodding vigorously. He was connected with everyone present and was joining in the fun.

Although children require some time to develop physical language they can receive the images and emotions of their parents and other adults because their attention is primarily in the subconscious mind. The subconscious mind communicates in pictures. The child can receive the pictures but they still need to learn the words of the physical world that represents the images. This is a significant part of the child's learning through the early years of life.

Adults use physical words to describe the images they hold in their minds. Physical language is a by-product of our existence in the physical world. There are many different languages on the planet, used by peoples of various cultural and ethnic backgrounds, to communicate. Even within the same country there are often different words to describe the same image. For example, in the United States, someone from the south, when offering a cold drink, might say "Would you like to have a soda?" In the northern portion of the country, you might hear "Would you like some pop?" The picture is the same regardless of what word is used. For clear communication to occur, it is vital that one have clear pictures in mind.

The picture language is the language of the subconscious mind. It is this language that transcends physical barriers from varying cultural backgrounds and ethnic origins. The picture language is also known as the Universal Language of Mind, universal in that the meaning of the pictures will apply to anyone, anytime and anyplace. A child is very open to this language from birth to around the age of seven or eight. It is at this time in their life that they have accumulated enough pieces of information that have been stored in their brain, that the child may begin to rely more on physical language and less on the inner language. This may be stimulated by pressure from friends or becoming caught up in the sensory experience of physical life. The end result is shutting out the inner communication of the subconscious mind and becoming engrossed in physical life.

The urge of the subconscious mind is to have a connection with our conscious waking mind and when we allow our waking mind to become so caught up in daily experiences, regardless of what those experiences are, then we may eventually forget about the inner Self.

The urge from within is very strong. When a child begins shutting out the inner mind, he or she will often have a frightening dream they remember the rest of their life. The subconscious mind will go to extreme lengths to get our attention. Its urge is to enlighten us regarding how we are using our experiences for learning. At any time in our lives, when we get so caught up in *doing* rather than *becoming*, the subconscious mind will give us a very strong message in the form of a nightmare in an effort to regain our attention.

It was around the age of seven when I had this dream.

I was in my father's corn field. Corn was all around me and I was trying to get back to our house. The corn was very tall, so I couldn't see anything except the corn. It was near harvest time, as the ears were full and the stalks were dry. Everywhere I turned snakes were wrapped around the stalks reaching out toward me. None of them ever bit me, but there was no where I could go to get away from them.

I still recall the dream experience and I also recall waking from this dream. My heart was pounding, as if I'd been running. I recall the security in the darkness, relieved that it had been a dream experience and not a real (waking) one. I dismissed the dream from my mind, calmed myself down and began thinking of what I was going to do at a gathering the next day with my friends.

Years later, when studying in the School of Metaphysics, I learned that *animals* represent compulsive ways of thinking or acting, of simply going through the motions with little thought. I learned that a *snake* was one of four exceptions to this and had a special meaning. In the Bible, the serpent in the Garden of Eden motivated Eve to partake of the fruit of the tree that God had instructed to leave alone. The snake is also wrapped around the caduceus or the symbol for healing used by physicians. The snake has deep significance. Symbolically, *Eve* represents the conscious mind and *fruit* represents knowledge. Eve then offered it to *Adam*, which represents the inner or subconscious mind. The physician heals in order to create wholeness of spirit, mind, emotions and body. The *serpent* represents the ego or motivator, which is the motivation toward learning through creative use of the mind, bringing knowledge and understandings to the Self. I had turned away from this inner urge at this point in my life. Running from snakes indicated that I was avoiding opportunities for learning and growth.

As we utilize our reasoning abilities for transformation, imagining improvements in our world and our selves, we are learning and through learning becoming more whole. The snakes in my dream indicated that I was avoiding movement toward becoming a greater being. I was becoming more interested in doing things with my friends than I was in developing my consciousness. I'd been very interested in learning through much of my early years. I had two older sisters who were always willing to read to me and teach me and I enjoyed this very much. However, when I started school, I had anticipated learning many things but was not really challenged and so I became very habitual in my approach to life, just going through the motions rather than learning which was my soul urge.

The soul is very invested in learning and growth. This is its sole purpose for incarning in the first place. Dreams are a way the subconscious mind conveys a message that will aid us in expanding our awareness and using our experiences for learning. Dreams are personal for the dreamer. They incorporate images from daily experiences into the dream. The symbols are familiar to the dreamer's waking conscious mind and come from memories stored within the brain. You must learn the symbolic language of mind in order to fully use these messages.

During the formative years, children often have experiences they do not understand. Growing up, surrounded with adults, who speak a language that is very unfamiliar to young immature ears, sometimes misunderstandings may occur. These misunderstandings may lead to fears of some sort. One man spoke of hearing his parents give instructions to the babysitter to keep the doors locked while they were gone. The youngster interpreted this to mean that there was something outdoors that might harm him and his siblings. This thought grew into other thoughts, where the whole evening was spent in fear of someone or something breaking into the home. He did not understand that this was simply a precaution, that there was really no expectation of someone harming him.

His dream that night was spent running from one dark place to another. Every time he thought he'd found a safe place, a monster would come from the darkness and begin chasing him. The monsters were very frightening and the one thing they had in common was that none of them had faces. They made loud, frightful, noises and had huge hands with claw like fingers, but he could never see their faces.

As an adult having studied dream interpretation, he now understands that *monsters* represented aspects of Self that he did not understand. These monsters were the product of his own imagination which took the simple idea of being sure to keep the doors locked and turned it into a fear that something would hurt him. In retrospect, and having had children of his own, he understood that his parents were simply wanting him and his siblings to be safe and secure. And if they'd had some idea that there was any danger lurking in the shadows, then certainly they would never have left them in the care of a babysitter. Rather they would have remained home with the children, protecting them.

The mind of a child often does not understand the intention behind adults' conversation and is fully capable of turning a simple statement into something that to an adult is irrational. The subconscious mind will reflect these thoughts and lack of understanding by altering a normal, human type of figure into a hideous, un-identifiable aspect or monster to illustrate the confused thought within the child's mind.

As children grow older and build greater understanding of the world around them, they often become more interested in physical appearances and relating to peers than in the inner, guiding voice. They may have dreams of running from something in the dark, something unknown. This reflects the time period in our lives during which we shut out the inner self.

I remember very clearly sitting at the breakfast table with my family and listening to my youngest sister talk about what God had told her during the night. I recall two thoughts that I had at the time. First of all, I wondered why God didn't talk to me. And secondly, I wondered why my parents seemed so astonished at this. My youngest sister had not yet attended church very much and our family didn't talk a lot about God in our house. We believed in God's existence, but did not have conversations about God. The prayers we spoke were at mealtimes and the prayer was always the same; a blessing for the food we were about to receive. My father was Catholic and my mother was Baptist, although not practicing. I grew up with an expanded perspective of religion, believing in the good of people of all faiths, but I did not have the personal relationship that my youngest sister seemed to have.

I had reached the age of shutting out my inner voice, the connection that we all experienced with the Creator. My thoughts of God were becoming intellectual, based on what I read or heard other people say. I heard what our priest said about people other than Catholics; it seemed they were doomed for purgatory. I knew my mother was a good person and did not believe she was doomed because she was of another faith. But I did not form ideas of who or what I really believed God to be. And so I was becoming more removed from the personal relationship with God that my youngest sister had.

Age and intellectual activity were separating me from the inner relationship that I'd once had with God. It was about 25 years later that I began once again considering that there must be something else beyond the physical world. During this 25-year period, I had few dreams that I can recall today. Once I began my study in the School of Metaphysics where part of the discipline is working with dreams each and every day, I began to re-awaken this inner communication. In the beginning, my dreams were pretty much the same each and every night. They involved houses, painting them, renovating them. Sometimes there were people in my dreams, but often I did not know them.

I'd just begun a study of the mind, and I'd spent a number of years being separated from my inner Self and so I was becoming familiar once again with my mind and with parts of my Self. The *house* represents the mind. And I was building awareness of the skills and abilities of mind such as undivided attention and concentration. I was also becoming familiar with unknown aspects of myself, talents and abilities that had been dormant for a while. The dreams in which I was fixing up and decorating houses was part of the re-awakening process.

After having studied for several months, I had this dream.

I was in a church which was filled with people. It was a Catholic style church, very ornate, with many stained glass windows and statues of the saints all around. In the midst of everyone, I began singing. My voice was beautiful, more beautiful than any voice I'd ever heard. I was very embarrassed at my singing, embarrassed that others could hear it.

When I went to class and shared this dream, my teacher said that I was developing a greater harmony within my spiritual growth, but that I was uncomfortable with this. It was like I wanted to experience it but not to let it be known that I was changing in this way.

It was at this time that I was really beginning to establish a relationship once again with my inner Self. It was new for me and although I liked the experience, I wasn't entirely comfortable with the changes I was making, primarily because these changes no longer fit with the choices I had made up to that point in my life.

I was driving through the countryside. We were going to view a house that could be mine if I wanted it. As we drove up to the property I was struck by the beauty of the countryside. The greens were greener than anything I'd ever seen in my life. The sky was bluer that any blue I'd ever seen. As we neared the house, which appeared to be a mansion with many beautiful gardens surrounding it, again I was in awe. I'd never seen such a beautiful home. I was thinking, this could be mine!

By this time in my spiritual growth, I had come to recognize many of the strengths that had been hidden to my sight previously. I was beginning to think of what I could do with these gifts. I'd always believed that everyone has gifts that can serve humanity and was coming to see more clearly these in myself. The thought that had been within my waking mind for some time had been of how I could be of service to humanity, and I was beginning to consider who I would become through offering my gifts. The beauty of the *house* and the *property* was an indication of the beauty that was within myself.

I was moving to the College of Metaphysics. I'd just arrived but had to go to some meeting so I left my stuff in the car. Following our meeting, I went to my room. I noticed that someone had moved my belongings in and I was very grateful. There was nothing in the room other than a bed and my belongings. I was excited about the prospect of decorating it. One of my teachers was living in the room next to mine. She was working on a painting. She was surrounded by light as she worked, smiling all the time. I felt that I was blessed to be in the room next to hers. I knew this was somehow going to aid me in my growth.

The *College of Metaphysics* symbolizes a place of tremendous learning and growth. My *teacher* represents an aspect of my superconscious mind. She was working on a *painting* which symbolizes the expression and use of the imagination. This dream reflects a culmination of re-awakening and beginning to imagine my potential as a Creator.

Each of us is on a path of revelation. Many of us shut out the inner, guiding voice as children. The subconscious mind has great faith and awaits the time when it can readily reach us and offer its guiding light to spiritual re-awakening. We have only to re-awaken what already exists. This lifetime is the culmination of many lifetimes of growth and progress. This lifetime is a piece in the puzzle of our existence as offspring of the Creator. Everything is valuable, for it is in the re-awakening that the truth of who we are will become apparent. The discovery of truth is what builds strength, and strength is what is needed to live a life of truth.

At any moment in our life, we can either pursue truth which brings us into the light of awareness of our nature as Creator, or we choose to remain in the darkness. Nature illustrates the natural movement toward light. Plants turn toward the sun to receive the rays. Insects fly toward a light shining in the darkness. Our nature is to move from darkness to light as well. The soul urge is toward the light, toward truth. Our dreams offer us a guiding light throughout all of what we do. They offer us the truth of who we are and who we are becoming.

Terry Martin is the Director of the School of Metaphysics in Champaign, IL. She has been studying metaphysics since 1988, is a graduate of the College of Metaphysics and serves on the Board of Governors as a representative of SOM Productions.

Intentional Dreaming

by Paul Blosser

I didn't think too much about dreams when I first started studying metaphysics. In the past 15 years I've progressed in the way I use my dreams, the way I understand dreams and the way I want to help people with their dreams. Dreams are important because everybody dreams. Everybody, at some time or other, has had some kind of dream experience they want to know more about. That's the great thing about a public service like the National Dream Hotline®. Every year on the fourth weekend of April, teachers and students of the School of Metaphysics answer phones around the clock to interpret dreams. Thousands, even millions of people listen to radio interviews and dream call-in shows and hear a dream interpreted, log on to our school website and find out what some of the common dreams are. It is a great way to educate people and let them know their dreams are important.

My intention is to look at dreams from a different perspective. There have been lots of books written about dreams and dream interpretation. What I want to present here are different ways to use your dreams. I want to stimulate you to move from a point of perhaps even being unconscious with your dreams to a level of using your dreams for intentional foresight to cause spiritual growth and progression.

I have identified a progression of thought with the development of how you use your dreams. This comes to light as you change the way you think, because you become more aware of your dreams and their importance. I will introduce four stages of dream progression; unconsciousness about dreams, consciousness about dreams, using dreams with intentional hindsight and using dreams with intentional foresight.

Throughout history, dreams have been mystical. They've been studied and used in different religious practices for insight and for spiritual awareness. The Native Americans would study and use dreams as a vision quest. If we look at the Holy books like the Bible or the Upanishads, there are references to dreams. For instance, Joseph in the Bible interpreted Pharaoh's dreams and offered him insight and helped him to understand the application of the dream.

Probably the very first metaphysical writings about dreams of which there are still written records were by Aristotle about 350 BC. He determined that dreams were personal in nature. The School of Metaphysics has brought that into the 21st Century and the 3rd Millennium with the idea that every dream is about the dreamer. One of Aristotle's students was Plato. He took Aristotle's idea a step further and developed it. He taught that the messages in dreams, the dreams themselves, came from the soul. From Plato's perspective, then, ever since man has existed in a physical body, we've had dreams. Even though we may not recall them, even though we may not be aware of them. We are a soul existing in this physical body, therefore we dream.

Every year during the National Dream Hotline® we do many radio interviews. Usually one or more of the radio show hosts will comment "I never dream, I don't dream, I've never dreamed." They do dream but they are unconscious about their dreams. This illustrates what I would call an unconscious level of dream awareness. It is unconscious because there is no awareness or even attention on dreams. This would be like driving to work every day and being unaware of the road signs that tell you what direction you are traveling in and where you are going. The road signs exist. The billboards are there, but you have no recall of what they are, what they say and therefore no idea about what they mean.

How does this unconsciousness about dreams develop? Two ways. The first is that from birth to about seven years old, a child forms his or her identity, separate from parents, siblings and significant other people. This is the identity that's going to be the essence of them as an adult. This identity is formed in part because the child's attention is moving more and more into the conscious mind. The child begins identifying with his physical body and his physical existence. The subconscious mind, where dreams, as well as things such as imaginary playmates come from, begins to be shut out. There is a dis-connection that occurs between the conscious mind and the subconscious mind as the conscious awareness moves away from the subconscious mind. Many children begin to have nightmares which is the subconscious mind's demand for attention.

The second reason for dream unconsciousness is as children, we are taught that dreams are unimportant and unreal. As a parent, I had this experience and you may remember something similar from your childhood. I was just learning about dreams as a new student in the School of Metaphysics, when my daughter was about 8 1/2. I heard her crying in the middle of the night one night and I went to see what was the matter. She was crying about a nightmare. I started to say 'Don't worry about it. It was just...' and I recognized my thought. I was going to tell her not to worry about it, it was just a dream, to dismiss her dream as something that wasn't real. But dreams are very real because the source of a dream is the soul, the real and permanent part of Self. It is important that I recognized my thought. Then I could sit down and talk to her about her dream and what it means. I explained to her why she would have a nightmare. As a parent, I began to understand her and what she was thinking and experiencing in her life.

With subtle lessons like 'It was just a dream' children are taught to dismiss dreams, to consider that they are unimportant and have no meaning. As adults we might develop the idea that dreams are entertainment or replays of the day's events or a result of something eaten that caused a bad dream. We might call such ideas urban legends or urban myths, since these are popular terms right now that identify something that is not necessarily based on fact.

Many people are completely unconscious of their dreams. But this doesn't mean this is bad. Here is the way dreams work and the purpose of dreams. The soul, the source of the dream, is always trying to get a message across to you about what you are doing. A message like "You're doing really well here. You handled that situation great, keep up the good work" or "This is what you were thinking today that didn't work so well. Here's a clue about what you can do different". Your soul and subconscious mind is like your best friend. Every night, it gives you counsel to help you be a better person when you wake up and to help you change the way that you handle life situations. So your dreams can be very insightful. They can be very good for you as far as self-awareness goes.

People who are unconscious of their dreams, may respond to their dream messages in an unconscious manner. For example, I get into an argument with my girl friend. That night my dream has a message about me thinking I was being attacked and I responded by defending myself. I don't remember the dream of course because I don't even know that I dream. I can keep going through the same kinds of experiences with my girl friend. Or I can do something different even with being unconscious about my dream. Here are two scenarios.

Scenario One: When I wake up, I recall the experience I had the day before and how terrible it was. I think something like "I can't keep living like this. I have to do something." So I decide to break off the relationship. Because I change my life situation, there is longer an immediate need for the subconscious mind to relate a message to me about how I get defensive in my thinking. At least temporarily, until some similar situation comes into my life again. Next time it may be with a boss, a relative or a new girl friend.

Scenario Two: Perhaps I wake up in the morning, not recalling my dream, and I recognize that I was being defensive with my girl friend during our argument. I decide that there are better ways to handle such a situation and that I will quit being so defensive. Even being unaware of my dream, I have made a change in my thinking and in my life that my dream was a stimulus towards. I have changed my thoughts and I have changed the experiences or situations in my life.

The first example of changing the life experiences is not productive. It is the way many people get through life. That's why they keep repeating the same kinds of situations in their life. You hear about people who go from one bad relationship to another, the same kind of job situations over and over or similar crisis situations over and over. Because they try to change things in a physical manner instead of looking for cause. Dreams are one way to identify cause. Dreams are one way to identify what your thoughts are and how, with your thoughts, you set up the conditions for those situations and the learning from these situations.

The second example I gave is productive because the dreamer is learning from life experiences. The dreamer is using those experiences to cause changes in his or her thinking and as a result the life situations change.

That is the unconsciousness approach to dreams and to life! There are many people who don't remember their dreams or use their dreams unconsciously. This is neither bad nor good. It is important to take mental action to be more self-aware. It is important that you are different every day because you are gaining awareness of your thoughts and how those thoughts relate to the situations in life.

The next point I want to talk about is where there is awareness about dreams, dream consciousness. There is awareness that you dream. There may be awareness that dreams have meaning. Someone at this level of dream awareness would probably recall a dream from childhood, maybe even have a recent dream. They may also want to have some understanding of the dream and given the opportunity would seek its meaning. They may even be able to put it into some kind of context with their life. Here is an example. A truck driver from South Carolina called about a dream he had over 20 years ago. He dreamed his dead brother visited him. Here is the dream:

My brother had died recently in a car wreck. I dreamed he came to me one night and he said 'I want to show you something'. So he took me to a beautiful place where I saw many people that I knew were dead. My brother said 'I just wanted to show you where I was. I wanted you to know that I was okay. You can't stay here, you've got to go.' Then I woke up and I was back in my bed.

The man wanted to know what his dream meant. He was looking for the meaning of the dream. His *brother* represents a conscious aspect or a conscious way of thinking that has changed.

The *other people* also represent different aspects. Since these are people he knew, they represent ways of thinking or qualities of thought that he was familiar with. The brother's message that 'you can't stay here' is a message from the truck driver's subconscious that he needed to remove his thoughts and attention from guilt or grief or any such way of thinking. It was no longer productive for him to stay in the same kind of thinking.

I explained that when someone dies, they may visit family and friends to let them know they are okay. I asked him if his brother's mouth was moving when he communicated and he said "No." I told him he had experienced mind-to-mind communication with his brother's spirit and that this dream was a visitation by his spirit. This made sense to him. He said he was the first person at the scene of the wreck after the police arrived. He identified his brother before they could remove the body from the car. This was very traumatic and there were many thoughts and feelings associated with his brother's death. So the dream served for his brother to contact him and help him to find peace and for him to remove his attention from unproductive thoughts and emotions.

So there was a consciousness that the truck driver had. He was aware of his dream. He believed that it was important and must have some kind of meaning. Given the opportunity of hearing about the National Dream Hotline®, he looked for knowledge and meaning. Finally, he could understand the dream in relationship to his life and what he was thinking and feeling at the time.

The next degree of dream awareness is how most people understand dreams and use dreams. I would call this level of dream awareness intentional hindsight. You know you dreamed. You know your dream is important and personal. You know that it has meaning. After the fact, you want to do something with it.

The first thing we teach about dreams is that you need to write them down. The reason is that your dreams are like an echo. In the morning the echo is very vibrant. The longer you wait to write it down, the fainter and fainter the echo gets. Also you have a tendency with the conscious mind and your conscious ego to color the dream, embellish the dream or forget things that might be significant. When you write your dreams down first thing in the morning, the truth and personal insight is there in the interpretation and application.

In this stage of intentional dreaming, hindsight is taking the dream and writing it down, interpreting it and then taking that interpretation and applying it in your life.

A grandmother called the dream hotline last year, distressed. She was concerned about her granddaughter's dream. Her granddaughter was home from school, sick because she was anxious about a nightmare. This is the granddaughter's dream:

She was tied to a chair and forced to watch her mother being killed.

These kinds of dreams are very traumatic because most of us don't have such experiences in our lives. We might see them on television or in a movie. I interpreted the dream for the grandmother. *Death* in a dream represents change and *people* who are authority figures like teachers and parents represent the dreamer's connection with superconscious mind, that part closest to God. These people in a dream represent a personal sense of authority. The *girl* is the dreamer herself. A *chair* represents a tool of mind, like memory or even perhaps decisiveness. *Tied* to a chair represents a restriction in the thinking, particularly in the conscious mind since the girl is the one tied up. The dream message is about a limitation in the granddaughter's thinking about how her authority is changing.

As we talked about the dream, the grandmother revealed her

granddaughter was a high school senior preparing to graduate. After graduation, the young woman was entering the US Army. She was making a major change in her life, from living at home under the close guidance of her parents to this whole new change in life-style. Her dream revealed her thoughts that she doesn't think she has a lot of freedom (*tied to the chair*) about what is happening in her life. The grandmother was relieved. The dream made sense. The dream interpretation gave the grandmother some peace and the information she needed to talk to her granddaughter about the dream.

It is that kind of application where you write down the dream, interpret it and then you apply it to your life situations that the dream becomes productive. And that is something that anybody can do every day. You write down your dream, interpret it and then look at the dream message and relate it to the previous 24 to 48 hours. That's how your dream is going to have relevancy because dreams are an immediate reflection of thoughts, perceptions and attitudes. So then you are more aware. This is what Plato was talking about with his idea that dreams come from the soul. Your dreams are a tool for self-awareness.

For example, a woman related the following dream that illustrates intentional hindsight:

I dreamed I was in a kitchen with a girl friend of mine trying to talk her into going to the beach. I'm not sure what area this was, but she had a beautiful beach in the backyard. The waves were very pretty and the sand was just gorgeous. And she was back and forth, she didn't want to go and then she did. By the time she made up her mind it was too late to go to the beach. So I was very disappointed. So we walked into the living room. There were two people sitting there and one, I believe they were married, I don't know. A male was laying on the couch and a female was sitting

*on the recliner and he was asking me to hand him his bathrobe.
It was white and so when I handed him his bathrobe, there was
a weight in the bottom of the bathrobe and it made it very difficult
to hand him this bathrobe. I finally gave him the bathrobe and
that's all I remember."*

One of the principles about dreams is that every dream is
about the dreamer. The other principle is that every person, place
or thing in the dream represents the dreamer. That's because
everything in the dream is personal. Your dream tells you about
you. Your dream does not tell you about your spouse or your boss
or your children. Everything in the dream tells you about you.
When you go to sleep at night, your subconscious mind sends a
message, much like a radio broadcast that is sent as vibration
through the air waves. That vibration strikes the pituitary gland.
The pituitary, which is one of the master glands in the body,
receives the vibration and uses the images in your brain to convert
the vibration into something meaningful which you can remember. The pituitary uses the brain images as symbols. It uses your
friend that you describe as flighty, to represent or mirror your
thinking that is also flighty, the way you can't or don't decide. A
beach in a dream represents the emotional level of mind. It is that
part of mind which is between the *water* which represents conscious life experiences and the *land* which represents subconscious
mind. The emotional level is what is between the outer physical
self and the inner self. The *man* in the dream represents a subconscious aspect. *People of the opposite sex* represent our inner
subconscious self and *people of the same sex* represent conscious
aspects or qualities of thought. Generally, those people of the
opposite sex are going to represent some way of thinking such as
the way you use your intuition or if you meditate, that person
might represent some kind of thinking that comes to you in
meditation. *Clothes* in a dream (*the bathrobe*) represent outer

expression. This robe represents a way of expressing your thoughts. The dream message is that you need to be aware of what your thoughts were and bring them into the physical world. Express your thoughts. The woman immediately understood the relevance to her life and how she could apply the dream. She said she had been experiencing emotional turmoil and in the process was starting to be aware of who she was and where she wanted to go with her life.

The important thing to remember about using dreams with intentional hindsight, is to take the dream message and apply it to your life. This is how you are going to benefit. If you had a dream two weeks ago and now you're trying to put it into the context of your life, you might still be able to do that if you can remember what the circumstances were otherwise you are going to have a very similar experience in your life again. If you can apply the dream message to your life then your dream serves as a stimulus for learning and causing the soul's spiritual progression.

The next level of dream awareness I want to address is intentional foresight where you begin to use your dreams to solve problems and to gain insight. Some people might call this dream programming or dream incubation. I spoke with a man from Louisiana who said he used his dreams to figure out the parameters used to select numbers for the state lottery. He called this dream telepathy. There are some other people that have done the same kind of thing. Neils Bohr, who was a Noble prize winning chemist, was researching what is now known as the benzene ring. He dreamed of a snake grasping its tail in its mouth. He knew that he could apply that dream to his research. This problem was occupying his conscious mind. His subconscious mind, through his dreams helped him to discover a solution. Albert Einstein had a similar experience when he was working on his theory of relativity. He had reached a block in his thinking and couldn't figure out what to do. As a result of a dream, he woke up and had the insight he needed to complete his theory of relativity. Thomas Alva Edison was another prolific dreamer. He put metal pie plates near an armchair where he napped. He would go to sleep in the chair with marbles in his hands. He would think about something he needed insight on, some invention he was working on and as he would doze off, he would relax and the marbles would fall out of his hands onto the pie plates and wake him up. He would write down what came to him in his dreams. So this is an example of being very purposeful with the dreams.

When I first started learning about dreams and metaphysics, I was vice-president of a small company in Norman Oklahoma. We purchased one of the first personal computer networks available. Top of the line system in 1983. We were having problems with the large database system that stored our customer information. The system was breaking down nearly every day or every two or three days. So I began to take the computer manuals home and study them. This computer system was very unstable because it would crash, it would break literally every day. Every day. Every day. So in trying to figure this all out, I would go home tired and when I slept I dreamed about the database crashing, day after day. What I realized, because of my dreams, was that I needed to do something about this. I needed to figure this out.

So one night it came to me in a dream with the database crashing, I interpreted the dream. A *computer* represents memory and memory was not solving the problem, either my memory of what the text book said about how to program the database language or our consultant's memory and expertise. I was trying to rely solely on memory and memory was not getting me where I needed to go. This dream stimulated me to use my imagination. I began to look other places, look at other resources, other people, other alternatives, to identify what we needed to do to solve the problem. And so it was a matter of being able to use my dreams purposely to find a solution.

Sharka is an artist and she was painting a picture of her daughter as a gift. But she was unhappy with the color combinations. She sought insight from her dreams and related a dream that helped her complete her painting.

I dreamed that a guide came to pick me up after my mother died and he brought me to a place where she was. She didn't see me or pay attention to me, but I was there observing what she was doing. She was really very happy, she was painting houses in the dream. She painted houses with these beautiful color combinations and I know that, I remember that when I woke up one of her desires was to work with colors. She was a sculptor and she didn't work with colors so I know that she was fulfilling her desire after death. So I was really very happy for her. In the dream, when I observed what my mother did, looking at her color combinations, there was one combination that was very similar to the color combinations in my painting, and there was one color that I did not have on my painting and she had and it was very balanced and very beautiful and that was the missing color in my painting. I remember that my eyes zoomed at that color. I remembered I was working on this painting and I'm dreaming that my mother has the color combination I need to remember this tone and I did.

After this dream, Sharka applied what she learned from her dream about color to complete the painting of her daughter. She was seeking a solution in her conscious mind and then her subconscious mind offered her a solution by way of her dream. She dreamed with intention and foresight.

Intentional foresight is the optimum way to use your dreams. A more elevated or conscious way to use your dreams is what I would refer to as spiritual intentional foresight. You use your dreams with foresight to learn about yourself. To learn more about your world and how you can become the true spiritual being that you are. What you end up causing in that light is very rapid spiritual growth.

There is an inner level celebration each year known as Wesak. This is the celebration of Buddha's birthday which occurs when the sun is in the astrological influence of Taurus and the moon is full in Scorpio. Wesak occurs in the inner levels of mind. All the spiritual leaders and religious leaders gather to discuss man's progress and how to further the spiritual evolution of humanity. Jesus, Buddha, Billy Graham, other spiritual teachers and masters of consciousness attend Wesak, anyone incarned or dis-incarned who is invested in the uplifting of humanity.

My first experience at Wesak was in 1989. I was surprised I was there and conscious I was there. But I was sitting next to my classmates and we watched people get up to give lectures and presentations. I recognized some of the students and teachers in the School of Metaphysics. My spiritual teacher had presented the idea of attending Wesak and I wanted to go. By stating my desire, by saying, 'I want to go to Wesak. I want to be a part of that,' I was there. I don't know that I would call this a dream because it really was an inner level experience. It was a pat on the back for me. It told me that I was doing what I was supposed to be doing, that I was right where I needed to be.

It is really simple to use your dreams in such a progressed manner. Before going to sleep, write a note to your subconscious mind. 'I want to gain some insight about how to be a better father' or 'I want insight about how to love my neighbor as myself', 'I want to know how I can be more connected to God, I want to be closer to God'. You pose those kinds of deep questions and subconscious mind works just like trying to solve any problem.

When you wake up, write down your experience, just as you have been training yourself to do with your dreams. That way you can cause spiritual transformation in yourself. It is good to write your desire for insight on paper. It affirms what you want and that what you want is going to come about.

I have been asking myself how I can be a better teacher. So I posed this question to my subconscious mind. "How can I stimulate the students, teachers and directors that I teach?" My desire is for students to be excited about their learning and spiritual growth. I want students to be invested in their life experiences, whether at work, as a parent, as a spouse or business owner. Many times students interpret spiritual growth or learning as having to do something. "I have to help at a fund raiser, I have to go to healing class, I have to go to class, I have to do my exercises". Anyway, I posed this questions before going to bed one night. I woke up early and meditated on the same question, then laid back down again for a few minutes. While I dozed, I had this dream:

My grandson, Devon was playing with his Mom and Dad. He was wearing white one-piece pajamas and a white baseball cap like his father wears. Devon is a very happy child and in the dream he was just laughing and having the best time.

When I woke, I realized that the dream was the answer to my prayer for insight. Devon was responding to the love of his parents and being with his parents. He was learning, he was loved and he was connected. This is how I can teach students. This is how I can teach teachers and directors, how I can inspire them. I can create experiences with them where they will learn and grow and experience the love and connection that Devon experiences every day.

Remember this. Your dreams offer insight and truth for you and about you. You can learn to use your dreams productively. You can be unconscious about your dreams or conscious. Or you can use your dreams intentionally through hindsight and foresight. It is a matter of you deciding to be conscious or unconscious about your life, about you deciding to be intentional or unintentional with your life experiences.

Paul Blosser is a graduate student in the School of Metaphysics. He teaches advanced course work at the College of Metaphysics and is the field director for the Chicago area branches of the School of Metaphysics. He has practiced and taught dream interpretation since 1987 and has participated in the National Dream Hotline® since 1988.

Dreaming for Your Health

by Mari Hamersley

For the past several years I have noticed that I am healthier than most people my age. I rarely get sick, have lots of energy and feel younger than my middle-aged years might indicate. I've observed that many people of my age (and some younger) complain about health conditions, notice themselves being in pain more often and believe they are losing their mental abilities. Having had an interest in wellness for many years, I decided to try to identify what I was doing differently than others were. I examined my nutrition and exercise. These were about average. And I never avoid being around people who are ill because I have little concern with "catching things". What I did notice that I do differently is that I seek self-awareness. I listen to my inner and outer thoughts through meditation and by interpreting my dreams. Then I respond quickly to their "good advice". This has been very beneficial in my efforts to live a happy, productive, and healthy life.

Having meditated daily for several years, I have come to know the peace of mind that it affords. Regular and deep meditation can aid anyone to experience and live spiritual unity within themselves and with others which is very conducive to creating a whole state of mind and body. In addition, our nightly dreams provide feedback from the subconscious mind. From these we are able to tell how we're doing in our daily lives because the dream messages occur for the purpose of revealing the conscious state of mind we've held the day before. I didn't realize the full import of these dream messages in being able to help us to remain healthy or to heal a disorder until an old friend helped me see it. And this occurred unexpectedly.

Through my participation with the School of Metaphysics, I am very fortunate to be able to meet many new people and tell them about what we offer at the School. This includes opportunities to be a guest on radio and television shows to educate people about dreams. One such experience really gave me insight into the revelatory quality of dreams as they relate to healing.

I was doing a Saturday morning show on a local radio station when I received a call from a woman named Cecilia. She had heard me helping people to understand their dreams and she called in to the station to have her dreams interpreted. Although she was put on hold for over 15 minutes while the news and advertisements were read, she held on the line. I could tell that she really wanted to know what her dreams meant. When I saw her first name on the computer screen, I received the impression that I knew her from somewhere. When her turn to speak to me finally came, I recognized the voice. She was a woman I had worked with 20 years earlier. Yet somehow she sounded different.

She proceeded to tell me that she had two recurring dreams in the past few years. In the first, she kept losing her car. When I told her that a car symbolized her physical body and her thoughts about losing it, she related that she had severe asthma and had almost become an invalid. She could hardly go outside of her house and her life had become a sad existence as a result of this.

I could hardly believe it, because in my memory Cecilia had been one of the most lively and vibrant women I had ever known. She prided herself on actively helping people to meet their needs for personal and career growth. While I was still thinking about this, she related the second dream in which the recurring theme was that she kept losing her money. This made a lot of sense for it represented her thoughts about losing her value, the money. She saw her value to herself and the world as that of helping people. This was the identity she had created for herself and how she had expressed her value.

In the short time that I had to respond on the radio, I was able to tell her that she is more than her body and that she can have value in new ways in her life. In changing her thinking about this, she would in fact aid herself to heal, to create a new identity of a person with value. She could begin having reason to live again. Although our conversation was very brief, I believe that she may have benefited from hearing that her dreams have clues as to what is really at the heart of her health problems. She certainly helped me to pull together the connections between wholeness in our thinking and bodies and how our dreams can make that awareness clearer.

To create health, one must understand the unity of the realms of life that make up the whole. Those realms are the mental, the emotional, the physical and the spiritual. Without the unity among these elements of the self, there is a lack or a misunderstanding. Used together by you the thinker, wholeness can be produced. All disease begins with a misunderstanding in our thinking producing a limitation. Over time, this weakens the body. For example, cancer, one of the most feared diseases in our world today, is caused by a hatred or lack of love for the self and others. This is a spiritual misunderstanding as well as a conscious one, for truly God is love and so must we be.

The cells of our bodies respond to each and every thought we have. Cells literally take their orders from the conscious thinking that populates our waking state. When recognized, these limitations can be replaced or changed as needed to produce different and better cellular responses in the body.

We create ourselves every day. When an illness or disorder shows up in the body in terms of pain, we simply need to have a more complete picture of what wholeness, or health is. This insight from the inner self is very needed and can be one of the best reasons for remembering and recording our dreams.

Each night the Subconscious mind provides feedback or a message, on our daily state of consciousness in dreams. It is up to us to recall and then seek to understand these symbolic messages. When this is done, the best orders can be given to the mind and body, enabling the cells to respond and make the right product, a whole, healthy mind and body.

Self awareness is the key. It gives us a leg to stand on for knowledge is power. With accurate information, we are able to make productive choices. I've always thought that it was better to know than to be in the dark, which is a state of a lack of awareness or knowing. Because what we know about ourselves can help us and because knowledge is power, then it makes sense to receive all the information we can in order to make the best decisions in thinking, the ones that will take us forward to living our highest ideals in life and creating fully.

To gain the greatest awareness, we need to realize that all parts of Self provide information. Physically the body shows us the effects of our thinking. In it we can recognize "signs" of what is going on. Symptoms show up here—the pain in the neck, the heart attack, the skinned knees, or perhaps even tuberculosis.

Emotionally, we might identify the painful feelings we have, such as sadness, depression, or apathy, as indicators that something isn't quite right with us. And sometimes it is a thought that comes to mind that helps us to understand that we are on the right track with our lives or not. Or Spiritual awareness comes when we pray or meditate or have a life-changing experience. All of the levels of the vehicle of the mind aid us to know ourselves if we will listen and pay attention. Because we dream nightly and often remember dreams, let's look at how they can be used as a diagnostic tool for health.

Since the majority of people think of their body when they think of wellness or illness, let's take a look at some of the ways that dreams reveal what is going on here. Thanks to Cecilia's dream, you know that a *car* in a dream represents the individual's physical body. This could be a car, a small boat, or a small airplane. (The larger vehicles, such as an airliner, a bus, or a large truck represent an organization.) In fact, dreams containing these small vehicles are often called health dreams because the condition of the car, boat or plane shows the condition of the body. It also shows how the body is thought of and is being used. In addition, they give clues to what is likely to occur within the body if the thinking is not changed. The body responds to the driver, the thinker's own mind.

A dream I had several years ago illustrates this very well.

I was on a freeway traveling at high speeds heading somewhere. There was another car being driven by an unknown person who was in the next lane. The faster I drove, the faster the other person drove until it became a race. I noticed the road narrowing ahead into one lane for construction. I could see that if one of us didn't do something different, we were going to crash. I couldn't get my car slowed down. By this time we were shooting like bullets down the highway. I woke up before we crashed.

Both *cars* represent how I was using my physical body at that time in my life. I was moving forward too rapidly toward my destination, my goals in life, and that I had pushed myself toward them at such a pace that my body was going to crash. I thought that I couldn't slow down. Fortunately, I didn't crash in the dream. It would have indicated that a pretty serious disorder would be likely to occur.

I had learned to interpret my dreams as a student at the School of Metaphysics. I knew that I had to cause a change very soon. I recall that I was quite intent on accomplishing what I saw as my duties in life. I had been pushing my body and could see that I needed to relax more and see things clearly. As I had been driving in the car, it was the action of the conscious mind, the racing in my thoughts, that had caused the situation. Knowing this, I immediately began to still my mind each day through concentration exercises and meditation. It was a matter of being aware of the state of my mind each day and slowing and focusing my thoughts so that I could move forward and respond in ways that I chose. It worked and I stayed healthy. In fact, I felt a much greater sense of peace and direction than before.

Another dream also indicated a potential health problem in a dramatic way.

I was at a gas station filling up my tank with gasoline. It was the same sports car that I mentioned above, a car that I loved. I put in the gas then went inside to pay for it. But before I did, I turned around and stood there watching as my car exploded in a ball of fire. It was totally destroyed.

To say I woke up suddenly would be an understatement. It was a dream that I can still see vividly today. The *gasoline* represents how I was using energies within my physical body, which I valued. And there was a great expansion in the use of energies, but it was uncontrolled and I was reacting to it. The dream indicated how I needed to gain greater control and to direct my energies productively so that I could move toward my goals in life.

Again I realized this and made changes in how I was using my energies so I prevented a health problem. Since I have never had another dream anything like this, I know that I learned a valuable lesson about how the mind, body, and energies work together to enable us to be where we want to be in our lives. We need to use these messages in our dreams with full awareness and direction.

A healthy body depends primarily on how the dreamer is using the mind. The emotional level of mind is the part of Subconscious mind that aids us to move our thoughts all the way out to the physical environment, so the emotions in a dream are important to pay attention to. Dream messages are neutral. The Subconscious mind simply and objectively presents information we need to know. Likewise, thoughts in the Subconscious mind are neutral. It is how we receive them as they move out to the conscious mind, that we give them meaning, seeing them positively, negatively or indifferently.

We create our thoughts consciously or unconsciously every moment of every day. Some of the things that influence how we think are what we have been taught as a child, what we have chosen to believe, and the experiences we have chosen to participate in. You'll notice that I put the responsibility for these on the Self rather than on others. We are the creators of our lives. Our inner self, the soul, provides opportunities for each of us to see to enhance our growth as spiritual beings in order to aid us to progress. Yet, in addition, we always have free will in how we choose to view and use those opportunities.

If we choose to respond to a situation habitually or compulsively rather than with imagination and attention, our Subconscious mind will often present animals in our dreams. Whenever I have a dream with animals in it, I take it seriously. I realize that this is where I am following habitual ways of thinking, or perhaps unproductive ways of thinking, that cause me to stay the same.

They keep us from responding fully and growing.

I was watching people play tennis with baby puppies for balls. It didn't seem to be hurting the beautiful little puppies as they were being hit back and forth, but I was incensed at the cruelty and wanted to put a stop to it for I was sure they would be killed. I didn't say anything though. The male players thought it was all okay.

In this dream, each *person* in the dream was an aspect of myself. Consciously, I was observing how I was challenged in life, both in responding to the potential change of habitual thinking, the puppies, and the desire to prevent this. These *(puppies)* were forms of habitual thinking that I considered to be helpless and cute. Yet my inner, Subconscious aspects I saw as perfectly willing to play with them. This shows the neutrality of the Subconscious mind. I interpreted this using the Universal Language of Mind to mean that I could use this type of thinking more productively and yet I was resisting this consciously, shown by the strong emotions I had in the dream. This was a time in my life when I was identifying who I was and who I wanted to be. I had to determine if some of the ways of thinking that I engaged in were to be played with or would be changed.

What does this have to do with health and healing? Habitual thinking is a pattern of thinking which has to do with what is the least line of resistance. It is often old patterns of thinking. While thought directed with imagination of who we are and who we want to become moves us forward providing the ability to respond to our inner desires. If we resist building this true self, we literally stop the growth and renewal within the body and mind. This sets up a condition where we are weakened or susceptible to illness. I knew I had grown in my thinking when I had another dream with an animal in it.

I was watching two circus performers on a beach near a city. There was a couple, a very tiny man and woman who looked liked acrobats or tightrope walkers. It was their job to gain control of a huge alligator, maybe 25 times their size. Heroically they did their best, and working together, they wrestled the giant alligator's head until they gained control of it. I was amazed.

In this dream I thought it was incredible that I was able to gain control of what I thought was a tremendously powerful habitual way of thinking, the alligator. With my Conscious and Subconscious minds, symbolized by the *woman* and the *man*, working together, I succeeded in using my thinking more productively and with control. This was a time in my life when I was deciding to create more positive thinking, even though I didn't know if I could actually do it. This dream showed me that I actually was capable of changing them and that I had done it the day before I had the dream. From it I identified a new kind of strength in using the Conscious and Subconscious together. I felt great inside and out. In identifying our own strengths, we bring about ideas that we are capable of change and this aids in bringing about a state of wellness.

Nightmares are another type of dream which reveal times when the Conscious mind is full of fear and worry. These are misunderstandings. They are states of mind in which we are in ignorance of what is Truth, and they produce a kind of stress that brings about a host of illnesses as a result. Darkness, or a lack of awareness, is often prevalent in nightmares.

I rarely have nightmares, but in this one I vividly recall how I felt.

I was at a movie studio where I was working. Clint Eastwood was making a movie, but everyone, including him, had left for the day. A truly evil man, incredibly heavy and strong with sinister black eyes and hair, hated me for some unknown reason. He blamed me for all his problems although I didn't even know him. Angrily he came after me and I ran. I got as far as the stairway when he pinned me down and held me and I knew he was going to kill me. I hoped Clint Eastwood would somehow come and save me. Then I woke up.

I was at a time in my life when I feared an inner part of myself that I didn't know. I saw this aspect of myself, the threatening man, as being angry with my conscious self and I feared this anger would cause a change in me. I wanted what I saw as the most beneficial aspect of my inner self, Clint Eastwood, to come and help me to overcome the anger and blame and hatred. This was a time in my life when I had to realize that all parts of myself can be used productively. The key was to learn more about the Subconscious aspects, because it was only the Conscious mind's perspective that what is within is harmful. The Subconscious mind only holds Truth. It will present that Truth to the Conscious mind for its own information and benefit. I decided how I would change myself as a result of that dream, by using imagination, working in a movie studio and aligning with an actor, rather than thinking I was unable to have what I desired.

Very close to this time, I had an intuitive health analysis done through the School of Metaphysics. The mental attitude revealed that the prime factor in holding me back from wholeness was a fear that I wasn't good enough and had never been good enough. As I received this awareness, I looked at it and started to imagine myself being able to accomplish that which I desired. Although it took a lot of mental effort to think differently at first, I persisted in imagining myself being able to accomplish what I had desired for a long time. I followed through with action and soon saw how much happier I was with myself. This eased the frustration and put me in a much better state of health.

To be healthy and at peace, to produce wholeness, we must

be creating. This is our reason for being in the physical. When we create with awareness and on purpose, our bodies have a reason for being. There is a newness to life. The energies flow smoothly, the organs serve us, and we feel great. On the other hand, if we are creating in ways that don't serve a greater good, or even if we refuse to create, our bodily functions begin to slow and we begin to die. It is up to each one of us to choose to fulfill our purpose in life. To do this we need to listen to what the Subconscious mind is telling us.

I dreamed my six-year old daughter had been raped by my husband's brother. I was incredibly angry with him.

This dream reveals how I was abusing my new ideas in my life. I was fighting creation at that time concerning a new idea, symbolized by *my daughter.* I consciously thought that an aspect of my subconscious mind was trying to force me to create. But really my need was to cooperate with my inner self and to create productively. I acted on this, and soon creation became so much easier, more harmonious, and more fulfilling for me. I didn't need to be angry with myself any longer. If I had continued to hold thoughts of resentment or anger that I had had for a long period of time, (and I might have done that without the awareness this dream provided), I could easily have developed cancer. Several close relatives in my family, including my own father, had died of cancer. Although it scared me initially, this dream proved very valuable.

At the opposite extreme, you may have had a dream which reflected beautiful love-making with someone you are committed to. This shows you have engaged in productive creation in your daily, waking life. These types of dreams reflect harmony that you are creating in yourself in using your Conscious and Subconscious minds. Think of the times when you had this type of dream and recall what you were creating. Also remember the state of your health so that you can identify and repeat the harmonious mental state. This is the a beautiful state of well-being in which you love yourself inside and out.

Finally, there are dreams that reflect a higher quality of thinking. These are the dreams that reveal what is occurring within our spiritual growth. Religious leaders, churches, and teachers, as well as governmental leaders all represent the superconscious mind, the most spiritual part of mind.

I was taking a trip to New York City. I started to go sight-seeing in the usual tourist sites, then I saw a church. I went in. It was simple, yet holy. Then I followed a hallway in the church which led to another church which was bigger and more ornate. I sat in a pew and simply observed it all. Then I left.

This dream revealed how I was exploring my spirituality, represented by the *churches*. I hadn't decided how I would use this new awareness yet, but the discovery of it unexpectedly was wonderful and peaceful for me. It was a time in my life and in my thinking when I consciously was moving forward and attempting to know myself as a spiritual being. I wanted to be closer to God and was meditating daily to realize this. Although I didn't have all the answers as to where this journey would lead me or how I could respond, I knew that I wanted to know more.

This is the ideal state of consciousness to have to create total wellness in our lives. We are spiritual beings in physical bodies for the purpose of learning to be creative like the Creator. When this awareness is part of our daily thinking, we develop a spiritual consciousness. When our attention is on more than our physical lives, when we have a realization of a reason for our existence, we truly are able to align with God and the healing abilities in ourselves. We are able to face any difficulty, to surrender any inharmony, to give our all, and to know that life is eternal. Then no thought or thing has the power to cause us harm. We are ready to build understandings which are permanent rather than gain information that is temporary. We are willing to create peacefully and productively, rather than feel anger or blame. We are able to love rather than to be in pain with the love that we are not receiving. We become whole.

All of this can be known through the act of interpreting the messages in the Universal Language of Mind, the language the subconscious speaks to the conscious mind. Dream interpretation is a wonderful diagnostic tool for your health. There is so much that can be gained from interpreting your dreams and responding to their messages. You can create a state of mind where every day is full of well-being. This creates health and wholeness permanently.

Mari Hamersley directs the School of Metaphysics in Des Moines, IA. She has been teaching and lecturing about dreams for 15 years. She often speaks to organizations about health and healing. Mari is a frequent guest on radio stations throughout Iowa interpreting callers' dreams.

The Key to Creation: Aligning the Minds

by Kathryn Gay

I went to David's house. It was a huge mansion. Inside we were talking. We were on the floor and started hugging and kissing. It felt good to be kissing him. I heard classical music playing upstairs. I wanted to hear the music, so we proceeded to walk upstairs...

Does this sound like a scene from a love story? In fact it is, it is the story of a harmonious relationship between the Conscious and Subconscious mind. This is one of those dreams that you want to continue for hours. This dream is the reflection of a person who in their waking life caused harmony with their inner self. In order for any creation to occur, you must have the cooperation between these two divisions of mind if you expect to create and fulfill your desires. The reason for this is because there is a symbiotic relationship between the two: the Conscious mind forms desires and the Subconscious mind aids in fulfilling them.

If you look in nature you will also find that it takes the two principles of aggressive and receptive to create anything. In females, the Conscious mind is receptive and the Subconscious mind is aggressive, and in males, the opposite. When the two unite, it creates a marriage made in heaven, as stated in the Bible. It takes a man and a woman to create a baby, it takes negative and positive poles to produce electricity. If we want to recharge a car battery we must correctly connect the negative and positive cables to the battery. If the cables are not properly aligned, then it will not work and you could potentially cause an explosion. So the key to recharging a battery or causing any creation to occur is by aligning the aggressive and receptive principles.

Everybody has desires and creations that they want to fulfill. Sometimes we create wonderful things and do not even know how and why we were so successful. This leads to uncertainty about our ability to create and fulfill our desires any time we want. By understanding how the mind works and how to interpret your dreams you can know what causes creation, and the intimate details about your relationship with your Subconscious mind. Each night in your dreams you will learn about your thoughts and attitudes regarding your Conscious state of awareness. These messages are invaluable tools in learning to live harmoniously with your Self and how to be a Master creator in your life.

The mind has three divisions: the Conscious mind, the Subconscious mind, and the Superconscious mind. The Conscious mind is what we use in our daily waking life, we use it to reason, to make choices, to learn, and to form desires. The next division inward is the Subconscious mind. Here is where we go each night to dream. It is also the permanent part of ourselves that we take with us lifetime after lifetime. It stores all the understandings built in a lifetime. Its duty is to fulfill the desires of the Conscious mind. It requires direction from the Conscious mind so that it can begin to use the Universal Laws and draw to you people, places, and things that will help you manifest your desires. Therefore it is necessary for the two minds to have open communication and a strong connection for our desires to be fulfilled.

The third division of the mind is the Superconscious mind;

the highest part of ourselves. It is here where we hold our plan for existence. It contains a blueprint for us to become a Creator. When the two lower divisions are aligned, you can then connect with the Superconscious mind to become one with the entire Universe. For now we will concentrate upon the lower two divisions.

How do we know if our Conscious mind and Subconscious mind are working together harmoniously? Next, how can we identify what caused the harmony? The answer to these questions may be found in your dreams. In a dream people of the same sex represent aspects of our Conscious mind, and members of the opposite sex represent aspects of the Subconscious mind. The interaction of males and females in your dream reveals the nature of the relationship between aspects of the inner and outer self. To understand what aspects of yourself are portrayed in the dream you must focus on the quality that the person represents in your waking life. If it is someone you do not know then it shows you are not familiar with that part of yourself. Get to know this part of your inner Self so that you can draw it out and create with it in the future.

I met a man named Jay who was studying at the School of Metaphysics. I immediately felt a connection with him because he had the same desire and urge to learn. He possessed a level of commitment that I admired. As my commitment to my spiritual learning grew, Jay began appearing in my dreams more and more, reflecting my desire to get to know this part of myself better.

I was at a School of Metaphysics function. I see Jay and I am glad to see him. I go over and talk with him. I notice he is alone wanting me to go over and talk to him. We talk and I notice I am looking at his eyes a lot. I wanted to find out more about Jay. I found a girl at the party and she started telling me about girls from the

School of Metaphysics that he had dated. She said they all took advantage of him. I felt sorry for him and thought I wouldn't do that to him.

This dream reflects my opening up to the part of my inner self which values commitment to spiritual growth. There are many benefits to surrounding yourself with new people, especially those invested in their spiritual learning and growth because they help you to understand yourself in a deeper way. People are in fact mirrors for us, so the more you surround yourself with other people, the better chance you have of discovering more of your own unique qualities. The desire for more closeness with this aspect of my Subconscious mind continued.

I am at the College of Metaphysics. I go to visit Jay who is lying on his bed. I realize I only have a small nightgown on, so I better change. I am lying close to Jay and want to kiss him. I leave and go put on a robe and then come back. He is reading with glasses on I say "oh, you are reading now?" and he answers yes. I am disappointed because I really wanted to talk to him.

This dream shows that what is inhibiting me from getting closer to my Subconscious is lack of openness and honesty. *Clothes* represent self-expression, so when you are naked in a dream it represents openness in the expression. The fact that I wanted to put on more clothing indicates that I was not willing to reveal and open up completely with this part of myself. *Eyes* represent perception and the fact that Jay is wearing glasses indicates I need to improve how I perceive this part of myself.

When you are not in harmony with your inner self, life can be very difficult. When the words you say outwardly and the thoughts you have inwardly are different, you may find it difficult to manifest your creation and you may feel frustrated that nothing is working out the way you want. The inharmony will be reflected in the dream state as a nightmare, or simply a very unpleasant dream like following dream illustrates.

I was in the shower. Sam came in the shower with me. I was furious with him. I told him if he took his pants off I would kick him where it counted and he wouldn't be able to walk for a month.

In order to cause growth from this type of dream you can begin by identifying what quality the person represents. In this case Sam represents the quality of passivity. I was angry at this part of myself that did not want to take charge and use the aggressive quality to create in life. I then used this dream to learn how to balance the aggressive and receptive energies within myself. I became aware of when I was being passive and looked for the cause behind the passivity. I soon learned to change this and as a result my dreams reflected the inner harmony I was creating with my inner Self.

And then comes sex...

If you deepen the relationship with your Subconscious mind you can expect to have very harmonious dreams. Sex in a dream feels just as good as it does in the physical because it is a direct result of the intimacy being created with your inner self. When a man and a woman make love it is usually the result of a deep love that has been built up between the two. In your dream it shows you have reached a deep level of intimacy and openness with yourself.

Sex in a dream is the beginning of creation. It indicates you are beginning to align the minds and use the creative energies to produce something. Each creation begins with a seed idea formed in the Conscious mind. This idea is then released into the Subconscious mind. The inner Self will then call upon all available resources to aid you in fulfilling the creation. As your ideas begin to work in the inner levels of mind you will move on to the next stage...

The Pregnancy

Pregnancy in a dream indicates you have an idea which is moving through the inner levels of mind. It is an exciting time! Physical creation is slow, nine months for the growing fetus to mature into a baby. Depending on the strength of your desire, your knowledge of how to wield the Universal Laws and your understanding of how to create will determine how quickly your idea manifests into your physical environment. In your dream you can see at what stage your idea is and how much more time it needs before it manifests! Is your stomach getting bigger? Are you arranging to receive your newborn creation?

The Labor Begins

It's the big moment - your creation is about to be born into the world. Wouldn't it be great to know before hand when your creation was going to appear so that you could make all the necessary preparations? Watch the progression of your dreams. They will indicate at what stage of manifestation the idea is, so you can begin to prepare.

What Happens if the Baby Is Never Born?

For several years Linda had recurring dreams of being pregnant. When she discovers she is pregnant she is upset because she doesn't want to have a child. The dream was upsetting for she already had nine children in her waking life and did not want to have any more. What did this recurring theme mean? When she learned that it was simply indicating she is forming many new ideas, she was relieved. The dream shows that Linda forms many ideas, yet when she sees they are beginning to take form, she pushes them away and does not want them to manifest.

The key for Linda is to identify the ideas she forms and then look to see why she rejects them. This is an example of someone who has many creative ideas and spends a lot of time thinking and imagining them, yet never takes action on them. Linda has the ability to imagine what she wants yet she does not initiate activity towards manifesting them. Linda now understands that if she is actually going to "deliver" the idea she will have to change her thoughts to produce ideas that she does want to manifest. When Linda begins to birth the babies in her dream she will find a sense of relief as her ideas finally manifest in the physical world.

What About Birth Control?

I experienced something similar to Linda at a time in my life when I was making a transition from my secure job as a teacher to opening up my own business. For two years I had been planning to open a holistic health center. I had a vision of a center where people could be treated with various modalities from chiropractic to acupuncture to herbology. I met other like-minded friends who shared this vision and together we began making plans.

As the time grew nearer to the opening of our holistic health center I began to have fears, doubts, and worries. Would I be able to make enough money to support myself? Did I really know enough to help others? How would I attract clients? All these fears began to knock down my self confidence, until a part of me began to seriously question this creation. I was not ready to leave my secure teaching position with a steady salary, paid vacation, and benefits.

My dreams accurately reflected those negative and unproductive thoughts. I began having dreams where I was with a man and we were going to make love, yet I could not because I was worried about not having birth control. I feared getting pregnant so I avoided the intimacy. This reflected my waking fear of actually manifesting the health center I envisioned for years. For it would mean a leap of faith on my part that it would work, and a belief in myself that I lacked. With the knowledge I gained from my dream I realized I needed to begin to rearrange my life to receive the new creation. I had to accept the change and have faith. Change had always been something difficult for me because I craved physical security in my life. I meditated upon the fact that the nature of the physical is change and talked with other people involved in the creation of the health center and together we supported each other as we embarked on this new adventure! When I began to let the fears go I found that things began to speed up as far as the completion of the building for our practice, and within months we were up and running.

Energy must express itself. So when you have an idea to create something it is important you nurture the idea and allow it to grow. When you form a desire in the Conscious mind you must release it into the Subconscious mind where it begins to develop. It is the natural flow of thoughts to move down through the various levels of mind until it manifests in the physical. Whenever this natural flow of energy is interrupted by thoughts such as doubt, then the energy becomes misdirected. It can result in health problems or some other type of misfortune. Look at how you view *sex* in a dream. Do you enjoy it? Do you fear it? This will indicate how you view creation in your waking life.

Another way people stop their creations as shown in dreams

is by *avoiding sex* all together. There was a period in my life I avoided creating by allowing my ideas to remain in my imagination. I believe I did this also because I feared that if my creations actually manifested that my life would be turned upside down. In the following dream I turned down a sexual encounter, the same way I turned down opportunities in life to create.

I am in the bedroom with this man. He is lying on the bed and he calls me over. I am afraid to go to him because I know he wants to have sex, so I tell him to go make some phone calls. I take some notebooks and go out of the room. I notice the tv is on so I start watching it.

Some people actually fight creation. *Rape* in a dream symbolizes forced creation. When the dreamer is a female and she dreams of a man raping her, this means that there is a Conscious refusal to receive what the Subconscious mind is offering. The dreamer is fighting the manifestation of her own desires. This type of dream is very insightful as far as showing you why you are not achieving your desires. This woman needs to stop fighting against herself and cooperate with desires that have already been set into motion. Remember that your Subconscious mind is simply doing its duty by creating what you desired in your Conscious mind. It cannot force something on you that you have not consciously desired and imaged. As you take responsibility for what you have imaged you will be better prepared to receive the manifestation of your thoughts.

Another way people sabotage their ideas is by killing them before they manifest in their physical life. It is similar to abortion, which in the Universal Language of Mind is the cessation of creative thought. When you have dreams of abortion, it is important to notice if you have been considering new ideas, but given up on them before they had a chance to manifest. Perhaps you have been rejecting ideas offered by others. Begin to pursue new ways of thinking and new ways of life that stimulate you!

Sex With the Same Sex

Susan told me she had recurring dreams where she and another woman were together in intimate situations. She feared this meant she had some underlying desire to be with women. The dream was confusing her so much it began causing her problems in her marriage. I explained to her that it meant that in her creations she was not including her Subconscious mind. It is very difficult and slow to only create with the Conscious mind. You are using only 1/3 of the whole mind! This brought to her realization that she feared the "unknown" and going within. She resisted meditation and ignored the intuitive feelings that she had. She constantly rejected the communication with her Subconscious mind. When she began to understand the function and purpose of her inner self, she began meditating. Her life began to change for the better and she found creating became much easier for her when she allowed her Subconscious to do its duty.

Broken Commitments

The ending of a marriage is a heartache for everyone involved. Likewise, the separation between your Subconscious and Conscious mind is a tragedy for your soul. When we form a commitment in the Conscious mind and then later do not want to accept this, it causes turmoil within. Once the desire has been formed and released into the Subconscious mind there is a need to cooperate with what you have set into motion.

I had made a commitment to attend a year long program in metaphysics at a college about 2,000 miles from my home. My soul had a strong urge to learn and grow in self awareness so I knew that I needed to go to fulfill this urge. However, as time grew nearer to my departure date, I began to get cold feet. I was fairly happy in my life and had created a life with a rewarding job, relationship and financial stability. How could I give all this up? I knew very little about the school program and was quite nervous about this. I battled over this in my mind daily, listing the pros and cons of attending the college. My failure to cooperate with what had already been set into motion caused nightly dreams that were quite upsetting. Each dream began the same...

My boyfriend Jim is talking with his ex-wife Sarah. I am watching them. She says to him, "Well I better give you a kiss good-bye" and she does. I am furious and start to get mad. I ask Jim if he still likes Sarah, and he says yes she is fun to be with. I say, "I can't believe you are with her again. You know she doesn't respect you. I can't believe you are talking like that - you aren't the person I thought you were." Then I punch him in the face, then I say I am sorry.

Jim's ex-wife represented the part of my Conscious mind that had difficulty with commitment, for in real life she broke off the commitment with Jim. I knew that Sarah would never be happy until she learned to commit and could then enjoy the freedom and deepness that she could develop in a relationship. She often dated two or three men at the same time. One will never find happiness until one commits to something in life. The dream made me realize I needed to make a commitment to my inner self so that I could experience true intimacy and peace within.

As soon as I focused and stopped battling with my decision to attend the college those dreams stopped. I immediately had more energy and felt a sense of relief. As I aligned the minds I experienced the peace I had been looking for. I began to create again. My meditations improved. I had begun to create what the Bible refers to as the marriage made in heaven.

What About Commitment

When you commit to something, the Universe begins to cooperate in ways you never imagined. When you commit to aligning the Conscious and the Subconscious mind for the purpose of creating you can expect miracles to happen. True commitment is when you commit to using the whole mind towards your spiritual growth and soul evolution.

What is sex without commitment? Are you truly committed to your creations? Your dreams will tell you the truth. Is your partner in the dream someone you are committed to? If not, you may just be creating for the heck of it with no purpose or commitment involved. I know what this is like, having a Gemini moon and wanting to taste a little bit of everything.

One of my friends approached me with a "get rich" scheme involving a multi-level marketing company. Although this had no connection to my ideals and goals in life, I decided to try it part time. I never felt right about it from the beginning, but went ahead. My dreams told me the truth...

I was at the school where I taught and I saw Gail, another teacher. I noticed she was pregnant. I asked her about it and she told me the story. She said she had been really good and responsible for a while but then she decided to ride the train for fun. She made her way through the train having sex with men along the way. I asked her where she was going on the train, and she said no particular destination, she just wanted to ride it for fun. I asked her about the father of the child, and she said he was in jail. I wondered if he would help take care of the baby. She didn't seem to be at all upset about the whole incident. *Others were calling her irresponsible because she already had one son out of wedlock. Christmas was coming soon so I thought about giving her some money.*

A situation like this will surely not produce a quality creation. I did not know the *men* in the dream and the *woman* signified to me someone who lacked purpose in life. The business deal in my life lacked purpose and commitment. The dream clearly showed me this idea was a distraction from my ideals and goals. The fact that the father of the child was in *jail* signifies that I have limitations arising from my failure to productively use the laws of creation. As I began to cause more commitment in my creations I began dreaming of marriage. Marriage symbolizes a commitment between the Conscious mind and the Subconscious mind for the fulfillment of desires.

I dreamt I was getting married. I bought the wedding dress and then at the wedding a lot of people were getting up to dance. People were dancing during dinner and I wished they would wait until after eating. The food was being served buffet style. I kept going back for more food.

This dream indicated the initiation of a new awareness for me. It was the result of my thoughts being more focused on committing to my spiritual growth. My commitment was reflected in how I was expressing myself (since in the dream I was wearing a *wedding dress*). The *food* represents knowledge, meaning I am learning how to commit. The result of my commitment brought harmony, represented by the people dancing and the music.

True peace and happiness comes with committing to your spiritual growth and soul evolution. You must be committed in your Conscious mind to align with the Subconscious and Superconscious minds. When your Conscious mind aligns with the Subconscious mind, you are able to create. We were made in the likeness of our Creator, so it is our duty to learn to be a creator like our spiritual parent. Creation requires the aggressive and receptive action. Using both the Conscious and Subconscious minds allows you to create. This truth has been spoken of in the Bible, Matthew, chapter 19, verse 4.

"..at the beginning the Creator made them male and female, and said 'For this reason a man will leave his father and mother and be united with his wife, and the two will become one flesh. So they are no longer two, but one.' Therefore what God has joined together, let man not separate."

Kathryn Gay discovered the School of Metaphysics in Ann Arbor, MI where she was attending college. She became a correspondence student while living in California, attended the College of Metaphysics for a year and currently serves as the Director for the SOM in Palatine, IL.

Existing On Other Planes

by Christine Andrews

"Joyce, is that really you?"
(laughing) "Yes, Christine, it really is."
"Joyce, I am so happy to see you! How are you? I want to tell you so much. I never got to tell you how much I appreciate you and love you ... I thought I might never see you again. It really is you!"

Thus began my conversation with Joyce Buchner in May 1995. She was my first teacher in the School of Metaphysics and had been a guide and inspiration to me for over a year. It had been a few months since I had last seen her and I had been thinking about Joyce quite a bit. What was most unusual about this conversation was that Joyce had died in March the same year. I remembered our conversation as a dream that was so real I awoke certain that I had actually talked to her. Although her illness had been drawn out I had not said everything I wanted to her and I regretted it. In my dream we talked extensively and I did tell her how much I appreciated her love and support. I was at peace with Joyce and myself for the first time in months. What I remembered as a dream was really an *inner level* experience. I understood that I had been with the soul that I knew as Joyce while my conscious mind was asleep.

I want to share with you three key *inner level* experiences I have had. I have remembered these experiences as dreams, however, they are memories of experiences I have had with other souls in the subconscious mind. Because the subconscious mind exits beyond the physical world we refer to it as an *inner level*. When someone has a strong urge to learn they will draw to them opportunities for soul growth whether awake or asleep. I have at times received instruction from my subconscious mind, much like my conversation with Joyce, while I was sleeping.

Inner Levels of Consciousness

Everyone's mind operates in the same way; how you use your mind is unique and completely up to you. Mind has three divisions: conscious, subconscious and superconscious *(see diagram on p. 116)*. Think of the very top of the triangle as the part of you that is closest to the Creator. From that point your awareness radiates outward through many levels of consciousness to the physical world. When we talk about *inner levels* it is from the conscious mind's perspective. The subconscious and superconscious divisions of mind are *inner*, closer to the Creator, while the conscious mind is *outer*, seemingly furthest from the Creator.

The conscious mind is most familiar to us. This is the part of our mind that we use when we are awake and experiencing the physical world around us. The five senses constantly feed our conscious minds with information. The purpose of the conscious mind is to learn and build permanent understandings through the daily activities that comprise our lives. Our planet is our school room and each day is filled with opportunities to change and grow.

Subconscious mind is the next division of mind inward. Often called the residence of the soul, this is also where dreams occur when you sleep. The function of the subconscious mind is to fulfill the conscious mind's desires. This is why the well-known saying "watch what you ask for you might get it" is true. Your subconscious mind will draw to you people, places and circumstances that are exactly what you need to fulfill your desires.

The conscious and subconscious are a team; they always work together. The subconscious mind responds to thoughts that populate the conscious waking mind during the day. When a person knows this truth and directs his thoughts toward growth, change, love, understanding and enlightenment, this is what the subconscious mind responds to. This is also true if you think about limitation, doubt, fear and insecurity. If you have experiences you don't understand or those that are difficult and painful you will want to investigate what thoughts **you** have been thinking. Thought is very powerful. Dreams are one way to become aware of the thoughts and attitudes you possess that are shaping your life.

The superconscious mind is the highest or most inner part of your mind. This is where the spark of life originates that fuels the rest of your mind. This part of mind is the closest to the Creator, the source of existence. Those who are Enlightened exist with full awareness of superconscious mind.

Dreams that are extra-ordinary are often inner level experiences. You remember these experiences as dreams upon awakening. The quality of these dreams is often described as "more real" or "it was just like I was there" and usually occurs at times when there has been or will soon be a major shift in consciousness in the individual.

Why Sanskrit?

I had recently begun teaching and attended my first National Teachers Conference at the College of Metaphysics campus. I believed this put me in the company of the some of the most experienced spiritual teachers in the world. I had some sense of what I was embarking on and it definitely awed me. I had also been practicing the spiritual disciplines of concentration and meditation for nearly six months. I was beginning to know my Self and understand how my mind worked. I was discovering answers to questions I had my whole life when I had this dream.

I am on the most beautiful grassy hill. The grass is so green and lush and the sun is shining brightly. I am struck by the brightness of the light yet I can still see all around me. I am sitting next to Dr. Barbara. She is reciting the Bhagavad Gita to me in Sanskrit. I understand what she is saying though. Her mouth is not moving and I know I am receiving her thoughts. It is as clear as if she is speaking out loud in English.

When I awoke from this dream I felt like I had really talked to Dr. Barbara. The memory was so clear and real that it was as if we had actually been together. The meaning of the dream revealed that I was at an evolutionary point in my learning. Following are the major symbols and their meaning in the Universal Language of Mind:

grass - subconscious mind experience
light - awareness
Dr. Barbara (my spiritual teacher) - receptive quality of superconscious mind
Bhagavad Gita (Hindu Holy work) - information about creation
Sanskrit - information about the structure of creation
telepathy - receiving thoughts mind-to-mind (in this dream Dr. Barbara was speaking but her mouth did not move)

I asked about this dream when I attended class that week. My teacher explained to me that I was to interpret it as I do any dream.

She then added that it was also an inner level experience that I had actually been with Dr. Barbara and she was teaching me while I was asleep. I remembered this experience as a dream since I had no other way to understand it at this point in my studies. Sanskrit is a language that is based on the structure of creation. I received this instruction in the inner levels and therefore the communication was relayed in its most "pure" form. If I was able to speak Sanskrit I would have been able to glean even more meaning from this experience. This was the first time I had heard of such a thing and I was amazed it was possible.

I had received a lot from the National Teachers Conference. My imagination was definitely stimulated and now this dream experience was revealing how I had also opened my Self in ways that were aiding me to fulfill my mission, and that included teaching. My desire to know the truth was so strong that I continued to receive teaching while my conscious mind and body rested. An important note is that Dr. Barbara's strong desire to teach the truth is what brought us together. Because I *remembered* the experience, it was apparent that my own awareness was increasing daily.

Taking the next step

Metaphysics was still very new to me. I was fascinated that it was possible to receive spiritual instruction while sleeping. This bit of information was helpful weeks later when I had another dream that was also outstanding.

I am at the College of Metaphysics. I am sitting at the table with Dr. Dan, Dr. Barbara, Sharka, Sherri and John. Dr. Dan looks at me and says, "You're here now, you might as well stay." I agree with him and ask Dr. Barbara what she thinks. She says, "You're ready to be here, I think it's a good idea." I decide I am going to stay.

College of Metaphysics - place in mind to focus on spiritual learning
Dr. Dan - aggressive action of superconscious mind
Dr. Barbara - receptive action of superconscious mind
people (Sharka, Sherri, John) - aspects of Self

Again, when I woke from this dream it was so real that I felt like I had been at that table. As with the other dream I thought about it often. I had considered attending the College of Metaphysics for a year of intensive study yet had not set a definite goal. When I interpreted the dream the meaning was clear to me. The essence of the dream was that much of my attention was on gaining greater spiritual awareness and as a result I was open to the highest part of my mind, the superconscious. This meant that my thoughts and actions were aligned with my purpose for this lifetime. This interpretation fit because it was true that my consciousness was filled with gaining spiritual awareness. Again, it seemed like there was something more to this dream that I had yet to understand. My answer came a week later.

I was talking with the director of the School of Metaphysics that I attended. She was teaching me about Wesak. Wesak occurs in the spring and is a celebration in honor of Buddha's birthday. A less known fact is that during this time all the souls invested in furthering the evolution of humanity come together as teachers and students in the inner levels. It is a time of reflection, contemplation and envisioning the future.

It is possible to be conscious of the activities during Wesak. Until one has honed the skills required to consciously exist in the inner levels, remembering dreams is the best way. I was curious to know if there was anything different about my dreams during

Wesak. Immediately I looked back through my dream journal and discovered I had this dream during that time and realized this was another inner level experience. Once again my desire to learn had brought me together with my spiritual teachers and I was receiving guidance from them.

An interesting footnote explains the three other people who were at the table with me. Sharka, Sherri and I did end up attending the College together in January of 1995. When I had the dream, however, Sharka was planning on beginning in July of 1994 and Sherri had no plans on attending. John had set a goal to begin his year of study in January 1995 but he was unprepared financially and therefore unable to fulfill his commitment. Our souls came together months before the actually physical event of attending the College took place and in some cases before the individual's conscious mind was even aware of the desire.

Because I had this dream during Wesak I believed it was very important and was willing to heed the advice given. My desire to learn was stronger than the limitations I had harbored. Within a few days I made the choice to attend the College of Metaphysics for a year of advanced study and I set a goal to begin in January of 1995. I communicated this goal to my teachers and backed it up with payment toward tuition.

Again, the people in this dream were my teachers so they represent, in this case, both the receptive and aggressive aspects of the superconscious mind. I was receiving direct teaching from them in the subconscious mind - we were not physically sitting at the table. As before it was my desire to learn and their desire to teach that brought us together. The powerful urge the soul has to build understanding and awareness truly goes beyond time and space.

The Fourth Level of Consciousness

A few years later I had this dream.

I am in a field and I run a few paces and take off. I fly really high. I can control every part of the flight really well. I fly up over the fence and above the trees. I circle around and come back. I land very gently in the field lying face down on the earth. My whole face is in the earth. Then I get up and fly away again.

The next thing I know I am in a room sitting in front of a computer. As I look at the screen messages appear. Someone is typing them in but I don't see who it is. I do see the messages though. They are equations that describe the structure of the universe mathematically. The translation and meaning of each equation is written below and it is in Sanskrit. I know this is very important. Lisa is sitting next to me and she is looking away at something else. I nudge her on the arm and tell her she needs to watch this because it is very important. I know I need to remember it. I print it out but only a portion of the text appears on the paper. I look at the computer again and think how important it is to remember.

Then I am walking through a house. I am looking for Paul. I mentally call out and ask where he is. From outside a window he says, "Here I am.." I am somewhat surprised that he answered my thought. I climb through the window and we walk across a field. It is night out. There is a white tent that has been erected. We look inside and Dr. Dan is conducting a ceremony. He is wearing a white robe. We join the people in the tent. There are people on both sides of him wearing orange robes. People in attendance walk up to him and kneel down. He places his hand on their foreheads. There is a giant fire at the front. It is awesome to see.

I awoke from this dream with a tremendous surge of energy and immediately was wide awake. Right away I knew this was very significant to me. As a student in the Advanced Series of lessons I had been studying the subconscious mind in depth for some time. The subconscious mind can be divided into four different levels. *(see diagram on the next page.)*   This is not a physical division; rather, it reflects levels of consciousness or states of awareness.

There are qualities associated with each level of the subconscious mind. The quality associated with the fourth level of mind is fire and this represents expansion. All the energies connected with this level of consciousness are expansive.   Because I was learning to work directly with these energies I was also bringing an expansion to my consciousness that was beyond anything that I had experienced prior.

Here are the main symbols in this dream:

flying - astral projection

face - identity

fence - limitation

earth - subconscious mind substance

field - subconscious awareness

computer - brain

mathematics - understanding of identity and relativity

Sanskrit - understanding the structure of creation

Lisa - aspect of conscious mind

house - mind

Paul - aspect of subconscious mind

Dr. Dan - aggressive part of superconscious mind

robes - outer expression

white - awareness

fire - expansion

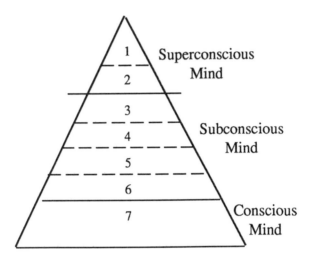

The nature of this dream was unlike anything I had ever experienced. The mathematical equations indicated that I was becoming aware of the inner structure of mind. As stated in *The Dreamer's Dictionary* by Dr. Barbara Condron, "Mathematics is the science of numbers. Numbers were invented to represent form. Forms represent universal principles. In dreams, mathematics symbolize the understanding of identity and relativity, two of the universal principles of creation."

The first part of the dream (landing with my face down in the field) indicates that I was identifying subconscious existence. This is true. I was practicing a spiritual exercise every day that brought me greater conscious awareness of my subconscious mind than ever before.

The ceremony in the dream indicates that I was at a point of initiation in my own conscious awareness. An initiation marks the beginning of something new, nothing is ever the same afterwards. Historically boys were tested on endurance, stamina, strength and bravery to mark the movement from adolescence to manhood. Girls attended ceremonies celebrating menses. These are examples of initiations that are physically oriented. They do, however, mark the greater shift of consciousness that occurs as one matures. For the spiritual aspirant there are many initiations that mark an evolving and expanding consciousness and this dream revealed my own progress.

I had recently made the life-changing decision to end my marriage and was adjusting to the direction I had chosen for myself. This choice stimulated me to think very deeply about my soul and what was most important to me. I had thankfully spent hours in prayer and meditation seeking Truth at a time when I felt great pain and sadness. My dedication was rewarding and I had begun to more completely understand the significance of these events to my own spiritual growth. I was using the experience to expand in ways that I had not done so before and the mental and spiritual work meant from this point on I would be different. Knowing the meaning of this dream brought me great comfort.

We remember the same dream

Over the next few years I dedicated more time to teaching. I had been a director of a School of Metaphysics and I was beginning to supervise more than one school at a time. When I awoke from this dream I was certain it was an inner level experience.

I am at the College of Metaphysics for our National Teacher's Conference. I am in the chapel helping to organize people. All the students from my Thursday night class are there and I am happy to see them. I look at Cheryl, one of the students, and ask her if she is teaching a class. She says, "No." I tell her that she must be teaching in order to attend the conference. She blurts out, "I want to teach!". I look at her and ask, "Did you hear yourself?". She said, "Yes".

When I remembered the dream it was so real it was like we had all been together. I recalled the dreams described earlier where I had gone to my own teachers for guidance and wondered if this was true with my students now. They were a close knit class and I was devoted to teaching them.

When we convened on Thursday night for weekly class I asked if anyone remembered their dream Monday morning. All of them nodded yes and I asked what the dream was. Each one described the same setting in their own words. Everyone in the class was together, there were a lot of people around and we were at the College of Metaphysics. Some students remembered that it was teacher's conference, some just remembered a lot of people around.

Cheryl said she remembered a lot of people and she recognized all her classmates. She said I was very prominent in the dream but she did not remember what I said to her.

This was important. Cheryl really wanted to teach other people what she had been learning. This was a very strong desire inside her, however, she was fearful that she would not be good teacher and consequently was full of excuses. This fear kept her from admitting her desire and acting on it. I had believed Cheryl's inner desire was to teach yet when I talked to her she denied it continually.

The way she was deceiving herself only occurred in her conscious mind. Fear is a product of a misguided imagination. When I communicated with her soul to soul in the dream state she readily admitted what she wanted. She even acknowledged that she was aware that she wanted to teach. Because Cheryl was not able to remember the specifics of our dream conversation it was clear she was still refusing to listen to her soul urge.

This dream helped me as a teacher. Any doubt I had about my perceptions vanished when I realized we had communicated in subconscious mind. I knew what her soul yearned for. This was a critical point for Cheryl. She believed in what she was learning and this experience was undeniable, especially because her classmates remembered the same thing. Unfortunately she chose to ignore what her soul was urging and never did teach metaphysics. If the conscious mind is unwilling to cooperate the soul will be left un-fulfilled.

This was a good lesson for me. I recognized the dream as a mark of my own spiritual progress and willingness to serve through teaching. My desire to give brought me together with these souls in this experience.

You can also learn to distinguish when you have dreams that are inner level experiences. I suggest you learn the Universal Language of Mind and interpret all the dreams you remember, so you can become adept at using this language of the soul. The dream experiences written about here occurred after I learned the Universal Language of Mind. This language gave me the means to understand what was happening in the inner realms of my mind. These dream memories of the inner levels show an awakening in my own soul. They are the very start of the awesome potential each one of us has when we develop reasoning and tap intuition.

As a reader of the Akashic Records, Christine Andrews aids others to realize their intuitive potential. As a teacher, she imparts the mental technology necessary to access the inner levels of mind. As director of SOM Productions, Christine realizes her dream of inspiring hope in humanity's destiny of peace. She serves as the Field Director for the Indiana-Kentucky Area of the School of Metaphysics.

Visitations *from the* **World Beyond**

by Dr. Sheila Benjamin

Have you ever talked with someone who has died? I have and so have many others. My curiosity about what happens to someone after they die has been alive within me since early in my life. I was not alone in this search. When I was twelve years old my friends and I would get together every Friday evening to raise the dead through what we called seance. We would meet in my friend Donna's parents' basement. The lights would be dim as we sat in a circle holding each others' hands. There would usually be someone in the group who had a deceased relative we were wanting to contact. Our minds would be still as we chanted the name of the person whose spirit we wanted to raise. Sometimes the lights in the room would become brighter and sometimes the room would become cooler. I don't know if we ever woke any of the spirits that we were calling; however, we did something. We were curious and wanted to know about what happens to someone after they die.

This experience stimulated the desire within myself to know more. I believe that it was one of the first experiences outside of my religious upbringing that gave me a taste of a more supernatural side of life. I did not know at the time that I would be using this information to aid me in putting together pieces of my own life with the death of my father as well as the important role it would play in my serving humanity.

When I was fourteen years old my father died. Even though I was pretty mature and understood that my father was free from the pain that he had experienced I had lots of questions which started my search to understand the worlds that existed beyond the physical world. I entered the School of Metaphysics in my early twenties and found that there was a way in which I could communicate with my father to find out how he was doing. My Spiritual Teacher at the time instructed me to ask my father to appear to me while I was sleeping in my dream. That night I went home and prayed that my father would appear to me. This is the dream that I had that night.

I was walking down a familiar street in my neighborhood when I saw my father walking towards me. He had a soft and warm smile on his face. I could tell that he was happy and at peace. Then I heard him say to me, " I am happy where I am. You and the rest of the family have nothing to worry about."

When I woke up from this dream I felt a sense of joy and peace. The communication that took place with my father was mental. When my father appeared to me his mouth did not move. The communication that took place was mind-to-mind or what is called mental telepathy. The Universal Symbol here is that when someone who has physically died appears to you the action which lets you know if their presence is really with you is when they communicate to you, it is done mentally. If someone who has died appears in your dream and is talking to you with their mouth then they represent an aspect of yourself.

Most of the time when someone who has left the physical existence desires to communicate to one who is left on the physical plane this takes place within our dreaming time. When we are asleep our conscious waking mind (the part of ourselves which relates to our physical waking world and our five senses) is set aside and our soul or subconscious mind is free to communicate to us. Those individuals who have died reside, so to speak, within the universal subconscious mind, therefore they are able to communicate with us directly in the form of what appears to be a dream.

I share this with you because many of us as human beings have a curiosity and a desire to know that our loved ones are doing well and most importantly to have some experience so that we can release the fear of death, our own death. Through this experience we get a glimpse of how expansive we are as souls. There are no limits as to how we can communicate. Through the experiences that will be shared by others we can see that there is a whole world beyond our physical senses that is waiting for us to explore.

We often look at our life here on Earth as being such a definite and final experience when in truth our time here is brief and for the purpose of learning. The physical existence is very temporary however, there is a part of our Creator's love that lives deep within our Self that is eternal.

As a child I was raised with a Catholic religious education. I learned about Heaven as a place where God lives. It was a beautiful place with harp music, angels and where you went when your life here on earth was for the highest of good. I did my best to conduct my life in the light of God knowing that Heaven was where I wanted to be at the end of my physical existence. I see Heaven a little different now in the sense that I perceive it as a state of awareness, a level of consciousness. I know from my lessons and teachings that within each of us is the urge to be compatible with our Creator and so we all are desiring to get to Heaven. I know that it takes several lifetimes to reach such an enlightened state.

Our soul is the part of ourselves which holds our understandings. We have built these throughout our present and past lifetimes. These understandings are permanent and stay with us always. We shed our physical bodies from lifetime to lifetime, like a snake sheds his skin. We carry with us only those parts that are understandings which will lead us closer to our Creator. In between incarnations we go through what people of many religions call a judgement period. Our life is reviewed and assessed. We determine what has been learned and what remains to be learned therefore preparing ourselves to re-enter the physical plane for our next grade or assignment. This review time can take a few years or many years to complete. It is during this reviewing time that the soul of the one who has died lives within the Universal Subconscious Mind.

There are times when one who has passed on through physical death has something more to communicate to those who remain on earth. Some people might think that the idea of talking with the dead is insane. This line of thinking is purely physical. The physical world is filled with limitations which do not exist in the spiritual world, which is limitless. The Christian Bible states that nothing is impossible with God and this is the truth at work here.

Here is an example of an experience that my nephew had after his great uncle Chester, who had died, decided to visit him.

One day as I was traveling with my five-year-old nephew, Michael in the back seat of his mother's van he began to share with me his experience and his insight.

"Auntie Sheila. I am going to die some day," he stated.

"That is true, Michael," I said.

"You and Uncle Brad are going to die too," he went on to say.

"That is true Michael, but we are not done on Earth with what we came to do," I said.

He said, "You know those that die can come visit us."

"Oh yeah," I said. "Does Uncle Chester come to see you?" I asked.

"Yes," he exclaimed. "He lives on my roof above my room because I can hear him snoring," he said.

This conversation was very refreshing to hear. My nephew at a very young age, had a direct glimpse of truth. The truth that communication is limitless and that there is a part of us that lives on forever.

It did not surprise me that my uncle would come to visit my nephew, Michael, since their relationship was very close. I believe that my uncle's reason for appearing or in this situation through the audio sense was to say good-bye to my nephew. My uncle, while alive, had a very strong purpose to serve and take care of his family. This strong pull was still present since there were many relatives who were still very attached to him and would pull to him. He appeared to the most open and innocent one of us all, Michael. Through Michael my uncle's message could be revealed and all of us could be assured of my uncle's safekeeping.

Oftentimes our youth are the most open to such supernatural experiences. An example of this was when Michael was three years old. At three, he was first introduced to death when his great aunt Jean died. He had visited her every day with his mother since she was providing care to my aunt as she was dying of cancer. Although the extreme emotions that his mother and several of the other relatives were experiencing and expressing were somewhat frightening to Michael, there was a place deep inside of him that knew that his great aunt Jean was at peace and free from sickness. My aunt Jean appeared to Michael as did my Uncle Chester. Here is the dream Michael had the night after my aunt died.

I was standing looking outside of the kitchen window. I saw a lady who was walking in the backyard. The lady was Auntie Jean and she was walking with Jesus. My mother asked me to call the lady in the house and I told her no she couldn't come. She needed to stay with Jesus. Then she waved to me and disappeared.

I had been studying for awhile in the School of Metaphysics and had a good open communication with my sister, Michael's mother. Because of this knowledge, when my sister heard the dream she knew that it was much more than a dream. She knew that my aunt indeed had communicated and visited my nephew. The peace that Michael possessed was because of the visitation he had with his great aunt.

The appearance of those who have died to those who remain is a pure act of love. Their purpose is to allow those who remain here in the physical to be assured that they are happy and at peace. When we are able to experience this we are able to more freely release our attachment, worry, fear, and sadness to those who have gone on. This release also frees the soul of the deceased. It allows the soul to freely review their previous life, assessing all that had been learned during that lifetime and evaluating what the soul may still need to learn. After this type of Judgement Day the spirit or soul begins to look around for a perfect fit, for their next incarnation in regards to geographical location, family members such as parents and older siblings, as well as astrological influences and the sex of the physical body. The important point here to remember and apply is that we must also let go of our emotional pull.

There was a study that was done a few years ago by a journalist who wanted to find out what allowed some individuals to live long abundant lives. The group of people they chose to interview were those who had lived past one hundred years of age. I believe the researchers were surprised at their findings because the major points had nothing to do with diet or other purely physical reasons but were mental ways of viewing their lives.

One of the four points that was common was the ability to release, to let go. I know that this does not always seem like an easy task, however one of the ladies who was interviewed said it quite beautifully. Her 70-year-old "baby" had died just before the interview was to take place. When the reporters asked her how she felt and if she wanted to follow through with the interview she said that God had given her a beautiful gift for the past 70 years and that she was merely returning her daughter to Him.

One of our weaknesses as a society is that we hold on to people, places, and things, far longer than is necessary. In relationship to those who have died this holding on can be a very uncomfortable place for the soul of the deceased therefore it is important to come to a point of understanding. In this case it is good to know that you can ask those who have gone on to visit you in your dreams.

Every year the School of Metaphysics dedicates the last weekend in April toward the education of dreams. We open our phone lines for 54 hours to answer questions about people's dreams as well as to interpret them. In the several years I have participated in this annual event there are always several individuals who call who want to know if the dream they had with their dead spouse, or parent or friend is really the loved one attempting to communicate with them. Sometimes what people want to know is how they might get in touch with one of their loved ones who has died. The Universal desire here is to understand and to come to some peace of mind.

Here is a dream that someone sent to us on our website:

I was having an ordinary dream one night about one full month after the death of my father-in-law. I was very close to him, he was more like a dad to me. I remember the dream so well, I can not stop thinking about it. My father-in-law appeared, or more like his spirit entered this dream that I was having. I was walking forward in my dream when suddenly I felt something strange. It was like a source of energy entered my body. I looked to my right and I noticed a large room. In this room was a dark figure sitting in a high back type of chair. The room did not have a door on the front of it, and did not appear to have a back wall either. It was just a large void. The dark figure was sitting straight up in the chair, the chair had nothing on the side of it, so I could see the figure in full view from where I was. For some strange reason I knew that I was dreaming at this point. I also knew that the dark figure was my father-in-law. I walked into the room, at this point of my dream I was inside a long infinite tunnel. The color inside the tunnel was white, but not real bright. I was communicating with him somehow. It was like I was reaching out to bring him near to me, but I never saw his face, I only talked to him somehow.

The first thing I said was, "I miss you" then I said, "are you happy." At this point he said "Yes," Then I said, "What is Heaven like?" He said, "It is very very nice," then he said, "It is very very pretty."

Our dreaming time is very important to the evolution of our souls. Everyone dreams and I know there are many out there who want to know if those who have left are wanting to talk to them.

When I first entered the School of Metaphysics one of the students who had been studying for a while communicated a dream that she had prior to her entering the School of Metaphysics which she felt is why she enrolled in the school. When she was a teenager during the Vietnam War, she had a dream that her brother who was fighting in the war came to visit her. She realized in the dream that her brother was dead and was coming to say good bye. The next day her parents received a knock on the door and two soldiers where standing at the door. The news they had to bring was that their son, her brother, had died in combat. For years she walked around with an element of guilt, thinking somehow she had caused her brother's death. It wasn't until she received some understanding about dreams that she understood how the mind has the ability to reach beyond physical location, time, and space to another. It was with this awareness that she could put her brother to rest.

I choose this example because this is common. Many people have been visited during their dreams by those who are in the process of dying or have recently gone on. At times these individuals who have such dreams feel that somehow they are responsible for their death when indeed they are merely saying good-bye.

Dreams have so very much to communicate to us as to the state of our conscious awareness and the changes we have to face. They can provide us with a depth of understanding that can allow us to be more attentive to our everyday and every moment experience.

I hope that the experiences which I have revealed to you have given you much to think about. I hope that it has provided you with information which you can use to add a level of understanding to your life and towards the relationships you have with others incarned and dis-incarned.

Dr. Sheila Benjamin has been studying and teaching Metaphysics for 23 years. She has earned all of the degrees offered in the School of Metaphysics. She has served on the Board of Governors for 17 years as the Treasurer and for the past two and a half years as the National President. She serves as a minister, counselor, teacher, and intuitive reporter.

Our Divine Nature

Dr. Laurel Clark

This chapter was excerpted from an address with the title "The Universal Language of Mind" given at the Unity-and-Diversity 30th Anniversary Festival in Los Angeles, California. The conference was designed to understand the underlying unity among seemingly diverse elements of society and to aid in creating a vision for a new universal civilization.

If you landed here from another planet and picked up a newspaper, what would you read? Stories of corruption, crime, violence, and disaster. Maybe a small feature about someone doing a good deed, but by far you'd read about the difficulties facing the world. Is this what life is about? Is humanity a mess? Whether you're talking about a societal problem like crime, or an individual problem like depression or loneliness, does it make sense that people are on this earth and live with problems? Surely that's not what life is for! Some people say, "Well, that's just human nature. It's human nature to have problems, it's human nature to steal, it's human nature to get angry." I don't believe that and I never *have* believed that.

If you read scripture from any religion in the world, if you read mythology or literature that speaks in symbols, you will find a prevailing thought. Every scripture says that there is a Higher Power; there is something greater than human beings. And these scriptures all say that *this greater power is a force for good,* it's not a force for evil. The other universal element in scripture is that people are made *like* this Higher Power that is a force for good.

Now it doesn't matter whether you call it God, or Allah, or Brahma or whether you don't even see it as a single deity. It might be the Buddha nature or the Tao. All of those names describe a single concept: that there is order in the universe, that the order is toward progressive goodness, the order is toward light (which means awareness), and that all of us are connected in an interrelated whole. So no matter where you are or who you are, one person's thoughts and actions affect everything and everybody else on this entire planet. That means that *we need each other*. It also means that what I do is important to your life and what you do is important to my life. And the more that we understand that, the more that we recognize how related we are to each other, the more everybody benefits.

The <u>Bible</u> describes creation like this:
"Let us make man in our image, after our likeness. And let them have dominion over the fish of the sea, the birds of the air, and over the cattle, and over all the wild animals and all the creatures that crawl upon the earth. So God created man in his image; in the divine image he created him; male and female he created them."
(Genesis 1:26 - 27)

That one passage gives you some very important keys to understand who we are, why we're here and why our true nature really is good. It says that we were created *after the likeness* of our Creator. That means that we were created *to be like* our Creator. Think about a child, a physical child who is created to be like his or her physical parent; they have similar attributes to the parent. Well, the same thing is true with us being created to be like our spiritual parent. We have the same attributes that our Creator has. That means that we're inherently creative beings; it means that we're inherently divine.

It also says that we were created *in the image* of God. The *image,* if you extend that word a little bit, is the same as the word *imagination.* It means that our creator imagined us into existence and that is also how we create, through the use of imagination.

If it is true that humanity really is divine, that we come from a Creator and that Creator is good, meaning that *we* are inherently good, then why *do* people fight? Why are they mean to each other, why do they steal from each other, why do they break into other people's stores? People do that because they have forgotten or denied the fact that they have a creative essence. They have forgotten, or maybe are not even aware, that they're not physical beings. We have these physical bodies that we use to get around in, but this physical body is not who we are. *Who we are* is a spiritual being or a soul. You know that by the fact that when you go to sleep at night you are not aware of your physical body, you're not aware of your physical senses, but you still exist. You exist in what we call a dream state.

As people become connected with their own inner Self or soul, they are able to understand why we're here and how to use this life for the purpose that is intended for us. When you're disconnected from your soul or inner Self you also become disconnected from other people. People become lonely, depressed, or angry because they are not fulfilling their own inner nature. When you are not fulfilling your inner nature you tend to take it out on other people which is unfortunate, but it still doesn't solve the problem. For example, if someone thinks that he doesn't have enough physical resources, and thinks that he doesn't have the skill or talent to earn what he wants, he may take or steal it from someone else. Do you think that really makes him happy? Criminals are not happy. People who are good to other people are happy. People who are loving are joyful. That tells me right there that our true nature is to be good and kind, not to be mean.

Life forms other than human beings harmonize with the world around them. They fulfill their nature because they don't have free will like we do. We have to *choose* to be happy. We have to *choose* to create. We have to *choose* to harmonize with one another. So there's a great blessing in that because it means that we can choose the highest spiritual way to harmonize with other beings, but it also means that we have a greater responsibility. It's not something that just comes automatically.

If you think about why we're here on Earth, it seems pretty obvious that we're not here to make money, we're not here to buy cars, we're not here to fill our houses with physical possessions, even though some people try to live that way. The reason why we're here is to know who we are and to know how we can become more like our Creator. In other words, we are here to learn how we can become more creative in everything we do. And to know how to love.

What is love? Have you ever had a plant that didn't seem to do very well and every time you watered it you thought, "I hate this plant. It just won't grow right!"? When you do that, in a short period of time the plant is dead. Now if you have a plant that's kind of weak and bedraggled, and you just love it, if every time you water it you touch it and think to it, "I love you. You are such a beautiful plant, I really love you," it flourishes. In a short period of time you can see how powerful that energy is. And that's not just true with plants. It's true with animals, it's true with people, it's true with anything you touch. Anything that you love you cause to flourish.

Think about people who are in love. When a couple is in love, everybody around them says, "You're beautiful, you're so happy. What is it about you? You just have this glow around you." That's what love is. It's a positive, creative, growth-filled force. It is the energy of God. And *that is why we're here, to create and to love.*

Now think of somebody you know who loves what they do in their life. It might be their job, or a church they belong to, it might be a hobby they pursue. I am certain that that person is happy. Such a person is a real pleasure to be around. He or she is also somebody who is concerned about other people. They're not just consumed in their own work, in their own hobby or in their own world.

When people are creating, they are at peace with themselves because they're fulfilling their true nature, their divine nature. When people love what they do, whatever the activity is, they are also at peace with themselves. And so they're good to other people.

The people who don't do that, the people who complain all the time, who are troublemakers, or who are engrossed in poverty, are people who are not creative in their lives. They are people who tend to live by habit or they tend to live for physical reasons only.

A good example of that is somebody in an occupation where they have physical goals only. People can be motivated for a period of time with physical goals like money, but it doesn't last. I have never met anybody who is motivated by money alone. I have met people who have been motivated by the love of their family or by a spiritual ideal. Speak to anyone who volunteers their time to help others; they're probably delighted to be doing it even though they're not getting paid. And that is true of most people who love what they do. The money is a nice benefit but that's not *why* they do what they do. They do it because they live for some ideal greater than themselves. And that is what all of us seek.

I believe that each one of us as an individual has some unique talent, some unique gift. There is something about each of us that is different from everybody else. Outwardly we can see it in physical differences of race, physical differences of culture, physical differences of religion and gender. But the real difference among each one of us is our own uniqueness and what we have to offer to the world.

I used to think of the world as being like a giant jig-saw puzzle and each person is one piece in the puzzle. When each person is doing what they're here to do this lifetime, if they're really giving from the inner source of their being, then we have the whole puzzle and it works well together. When people don't know why they are here or they deny why they are here — sometimes people do have some idea of their gifts but they don't use them for a variety of reasons — that's when they take away from the puzzle. It's when they think they have to grab more than is theirs, or when they get jealous of other people and try to tear down other people. So the real solution for us to live in harmony with all of our differences is for each one of us to do what we're here to do, what is fulfilling to our souls. When you do that, you know that physical things are not what make you happy.

Sometimes people believe that there is more to life than just acquiring physical possessions. But they don't always know how to find out what that is. There are two ways that will always work to connect with your own inner Self, to find out why you are here and how to do it. The first way is through stilling your mind through some kind of spiritual discipline like concentration, and then cultivating inner listening with meditation. When you can still the chatter in your conscious mind, when you can still the thoughts that go racing through your mind all the time and really *hear* your Inner Self, that in itself will transform your life.

The second way is through understanding your dreams, the dreams that you have at night. Every night when we go to sleep we shut off the chatter in our conscious mind. When you're asleep you're not aware of your physical body, you're not aware of your physical senses, you're not distracted by the fifty billion physical desires that are around you. All of that is shut off, and the part of you that you can be aware of is called your soul or your Inner Self.

Your dreams are a communication, from your Inner Self or your soul to your outer self or your conscious mind, that tell you about you. Every dream that you have tells you about you. And when I say *you* I'm not talking about the physical you; I'm talking about the *soul* you. Your dreams tell you about the state of your own awareness. They will tell you about what is most productive and fulfilling to your soul and will give you very specific guidance to understand how to fulfill that.

In order to learn how to use those messages it means understanding the language that your dreams speak, and that language is a language of symbols. It's what in the School of Metaphysics we have termed the Universal Language of Mind. The "universal" part of the Universal Language of Mind means that the symbols are universal. They mean the same thing for everyone no matter who they are, no matter where they're from, no matter what their background is.

When you read mythology or scripture, you'll find that the same myths and the same stories in scripture show up in all cultures, in any language, whatever group of people it relates to. Even though the names of people are different and the outward trappings might be a little bit different, the same images run through all scriptures and through all mythology, even fairy tales. Now, why is that? It's because the language of images or symbols is universal. And it is also because at a soul level all of us are connected. We all have universal desires, we all have universal urges, we all have the same reason for being here despite our outward physical differences.

In college I studied philosophy. I remember reading Plato and his idea of Forms. The idea is that for every physical object that exists in the universe there is a Form in the inner levels of consciousness. That idea was so stimulating to me, but I really didn't understand it. When I learned about the Universal Language of Mind I began to understand what he was talking about. Every physical thing in this world is an outward manifestation of an inner soul desire or an inner soul need. The *inner essence* of every physical thing is the reason why we even have desires. Any spiritual teacher understands that and that's why spiritual teachings, for the most part, are told in stories. They're told in allegories, they're told in parables, because those are pictures. A picture is universal, something that anyone can relate to.

When you see a street sign with an arrow pointing left, in a red circle with a slash through it, what does that picture mean? "No left turn." Now if you did not speak English as your native language, you would still know that means "no left turn." That is why symbols are used for street signs, because you don't have to be able to read, you don't have to be able to speak a particular physical language to understand it. In the cars we drive nowadays it doesn't say the word "seatbelt"; you have a little picture of a man with a seatbelt on. The picture is universal and that is the Universal Language of Mind, a language of symbols or images. It's why "user friendly" computers have little icons — they're pictures so that you can understand what those commands are telling you.

The same thing is true of the Universal Language of Mind as it appears in scripture, as it appears in mythology, as it appears in your dreams. If you understand what those symbols mean then you can understand any scripture, you can understand any myth, you can understand your own Self through your dreams. So it's a very valuable language to understand and know.

One of the most appealing things to me about understanding the Universal Language of Mind is that it helps you to understand why you have the kinds of physical desires that you have. It helps you to understand that we do all come from a common origin. We come from the same source and we are all going to the same place. We're all going toward each one of us fulfilling our complete potential, being completely divine if you want to call it that. The more we understand what our physical desires are telling us about our soul desires, the simpler it is for us to fulfill them. Then we can be at peace with ourselves and be at peace with one another. If you talk to people from different backgrounds and different cultures, you'll find out that people want essentially the same things.

People have universal desires. Learning what people want and why they want it helps us to live more fulfilled lives. I'll give you an example. Many people nowadays want money. Some people want a lot of money. Some people want just enough money to care for their needs but everybody wants money. Why? Think about where money came from and how it was developed; it is a means of exchange that we use to represent our own value. When you work, you give something of value—your talent, your creativity, physical labor, reasoning skills, service — to others who want it. They pay you for investing yourself and your time. In most cases, the money that you receive you then exchange for something of value possessed by someone else. Let's say someone is an artist who makes jewelry and sells it. They have created something of value. You grow corn and sell it. The money you receive for your corn (which is valuable to the person who buys it) you use to buy the jewelry. Essentially you are trading the value you have invested in producing corn for the value the artist has invested in crafting the jewelry. So money is an exchange of value.

The inner reason why people want money is because they want to understand their own value. That is the reason why people who do volunteer work that they know is valuable are not so concerned about whether they get paid for it. They don't need the symbol of money to let them know that they are valuable. They know it because they know that they are doing good works. One of my ideals is that everybody will give of themselves so they know they are valuable whether or not they receive money for it.

Now think about somebody who never has enough money; no matter how much money they have, they think it's never enough. They could have a million dollars and it's not enough or they could have five dollars and it's not enough. Some people never believe that what they have is enough. Those people do not know their own value. They don't understand what it is about them that is valuable. I remember talking to one such woman, telling her some of the things that I really appreciated about her, and she didn't believe me. She did not believe that those were actually qualities in herself! So it began to make sense to me why this person also never seems to think that the money that she has is enough, because she is not aware of how valuable she is as a person.

When people know that *money* symbolizes value and understand that, then they can begin to put the desire for money into perspective. Many people think that one of the problems we have these days is that there are not enough resources to go around; for the number of people we have on this planet there are not enough physical resources. Their idea is that this universe is a pie that has a fixed number of pieces. So if you have ten people and there's only eight pieces of the pie, there's not enough to go around. But on a spiritual level that is not true. We have abundant resources and the more creative we are the better use we make of the resources we have.

On a physical level you can see how that happens when you have finished with a piece of clothing you have worn, it's still in good condition and you donate it to a charity so someone else gets to wear it. That physical resource has been used for more than one person. Or when you make something with your hands rather than buying it; that is another way to more completely use resources. There are many ways that we can become more resourceful. Probably the best way to discover that there is more than enough for everyone on this planet is to eliminate waste. If you, in even small ways, eliminate the amount of resources that you waste, if you don't use up as much because you don't really need it, then that's available for someone else to use. When you produce more than you consume, then you contribute to greater abundance for everyone.

The more that you learn how to find soul fulfillment, the more you discover the difference between what you really *need* to be fulfilled and what you want. There are unlimited physical desires that you could satisfy, and if all you think about are your physical desires, without thinking about what those represent in terms of your soul needs, then you're never satisfied. For example, you buy a car and there are ten more new cars that come out, so you could want ten more new cars, or you buy an article of clothing, then there are fifty thousand other articles of clothing that you could buy. When you think about what you *need* and you satisfy that need, there's plenty, there's more than plenty to be fulfilled. And that is what the Universal Language of Mind can help you to understand. *What does this physical thing represent to me as a soul and how can I fulfill that soul desire?*

Another illustration of how the Universal Language of Mind can help us derive greater meaning from life is understanding what it symbolizes when *other people* in your life show up in your dreams. Think about the people who you know who you're drawn to or attracted to; you are not physically attracted to them even though you might think of it that way. You're drawn to a quality *within* that person that you admire, and probably one that you want to make a part of your own expression. Perhaps you choose to be around people who are magnanimous and generous. You enjoy them because you appreciate those characteristics. Now think about the flip side of that, a person who just gets under your skin. There is a quality *in* them that irritates you, and although most people don't like to admit it, in most cases that is a quality in you as well.

The more that you learn to understand yourself, and how to understand those qualities *in yourself* that are a source of conflict, the more you harmonize with other people. You have fewer conflicts with other people. This is one of the most valuable lessons that you can learn from your dreams, because we have discovered in our research in the School of Metaphysics that when you dream about other people you're not really dreaming about other people. Those people in your dreams symbolize aspects or qualities in yourself so you're dreaming about *you* when you dream about those other people.

Sometimes people don't want to admit that other people symbolize aspects of themselves. They say "Oh no, no, there's no way I'm like my ex-husband!" But they dream about him all the time. What they're dreaming about is a part of themselves that they want to understand. And the beautiful thing about that is when you *do* admit that those qualities are in you, and you learn to understand them and transform them in yourself, it transforms your relationships with other people.

When I first started studying metaphysics I was pretty passive and indecisive outwardly. I had strong ideas and convictions but I would never speak my mind. And I could not understand why throughout my life I was around people who were really bossy and domineering who would always tell me what to do. Well, the fact is, I wanted to incorporate into myself being more decisive and being more directive. But I wasn't doing that, so I kept choosing to be in situations with people who would tell me what to do, because I wasn't deciding for myself what I wanted to do. When I finally admitted that and started changing some of the passivity by being more directive, lo and behold, I found that those people didn't bug me so much any more. I didn't find so much anymore that they seemed bossy and domineering. And I also found that I was able to get along with them better because I was speaking my mind more and I didn't let them push me around and they didn't try to push me around. You probably have heard this idea before: people do not become victimized by accident. People bring it upon themselves. It may be hard to admit that, but when you do admit and change it, then your life really changes and your relationships with other people change.

When you can interpret what the experiences and events in your physical world represent to you as a soul, you can cause transformation in yourself. You can understand how to make choices that will be productive and fulfilling for your Self. One of the reasons why the School of Metaphysics was brought into being was to teach people how to understand the Universal Language of Mind. Throughout history there have been many cultures that have understood the value of dreams. In many cultures the only people who interpret dreams are the holy people like the priests or the shamans. The same thing is true with scripture interpretation. In some religions only the priests or the ministers or the rabbis interpret the scriptures.

Part of our mission in the School of Metaphysics is to teach everyone about the Universal Language of Mind, so that what have previously been *inner secrets* of the mind and the Self are not secret any more, so that everybody can understand, so that everybody can become more fulfilled and productive. When you cause peace within your Self it causes peace among other people. We are committed to the ideal of causing that to come about.

The word *education* means to draw forth. A good teacher is one who gives you guidance and direction, enabling you to draw forth from within yourself your own potential. That's true education, to draw forth from within the individual what they already have inside. Learning to interpret dreams is like having a teacher at your bedside, enabling you to draw forth, develop, use, and fulfill your full potential. Then you can bring about the fulfillment and fruition of what is divine within yourself.•

Laurel Clark, D.D., D.M., is a teacher, ordained minister, and counselor. She has been teaching dreams and related aspects of applied metaphysics since 1979. An accomplished public speaker, she speaks to organizations, universities, businesses, hospitals and other groups on many applications of metaphysics for better living.
Laurel mentors Spiritual Focus Weekend retreats on the campus of the College of Metaphysics, including one in the fall called "Manifest Destiny: Fulfilling Your Soul's Purpose."

www.dreamschool.org's

Dream of the Month

Learning to interpret your dreams is like learning a new language. You have a means to communicate your thoughts to others that was previously out of your reach. Everyone dreams, just as most everyone speaks and hears. To wield language, we learn how to read and write. To understand the meaning in dream communications, we learn mental skills of concentration, recall, and reasoning. These then become the foundation for lucid dreaming and eventually transcendent awareness.

We share much of our research into humanity's potential through the Internet. Our virtual campus at www.som.org has a sister campus devoted entirely to dream study. Here you will find transcripts of interviews, lessons, and chats with the foremost authorities in this field. You can receive lessons for study in your own home. By visiting www.dreamschool.org, you have thousands of questions answered, hundreds of dream symbols at your fingertips and dozens of dreams interpreted.

One of the many e-mail dreams we receive is chosen each month for interpretation by instructors at the College of Metaphysics. We call this *Dream of the Month.* A longer, more detailed dream offers great insight into the benefit of remembering, recording, interpreting, and responding to these subconscious messages. Dozens of dreams can be accessed on our site to help you learn about your own.

To have your dreams interpreted via our Internet campus, you may e-mail us at som@som.org. Other resources for learning how to interpret your dreams are listed on the following page.

The most complete understanding and application of the principles of interpreting dreams is gained through our course of study in metaphysics.

For home study...School of Metaphysics titles

Books
The Dreamer's Dictionary by Barbara Condron
Every Dream is about the Dreamer by B. Condron
The Bible Interpreted in Dream Symbols
        by Condron, Condron, Matthes, Rothermel
Dreams of the Soul by Daniel R. Condron
Understanding Your Dreams by Daniel R. Condron
25 Most Commonly Asked Questions About Dreams
by SOM Faculty

Books on Tape
Mechanics of Dreams by J. Rothermel $12.00
Dreams: Language of the Soul by J. Rothermel $8.00
Symbols of Dreams by J. Rothermel $12.00
Who are Those Strangers in My Dreams?
        by B. Condron $12.00

Audio Cassette Tapes ($8 each)
Five Steps of Creative Dreaming by Dr. B. Condron
Spiritual Science of Dreaming by Dr. Barbara Condron
Universal Language of Mind by Dr. Daniel Condron
Dreams: Inner Communication by Paul Blosser

Eight Lesson Course
Dreamschool $40.00
Nocturnal Visions (VHS) $20.00
A World of Dreams (VHS) $20.00

coming soon
Dreaming as an Altered State of Consciousness

Additional titles available from SOM Publishing include:

Karmic Healing
Dr. Laurel Clark ISBN: 0944386-26-1 $15.00

The Bible Interpreted in Dream Symbols
Drs. Condron, Condron, Matthes, Rothermel
ISBN: 0944386-23-7 $18.00

Spiritual Renaissance
Elevating Your Conciousness for the Common Good
Dr. Barbara Condron   ISBN: 0944386-22-9 $15.00

Superconscious Meditation
Kundalini & the Understanding of the Whole Mind
Dr. Daniel R. Condron ISBN 0944386-21-0 $13.00

First Opinion: Wholistic Health Care in the 21st Century
Dr. Barbara Condron ISBN 0944386-18-0 $15.00

The Dreamer's Dictionary
Dr. Barbara Condron ISBN 0944386-16-4 $15.00

The Work of the Soul
Dr. Barbara Condron, ed. ISBN 0944386-17-2 $13.00

Uncommon Knowledge   Past Life & Health Readings
Dr. Barbara Condron, ed. ISBN 0944386-19-9 $13.00

The Universal Language of Mind
The Book of Matthew Interpreted
Dr. Daniel R. Condron ISBN 0944386-15-6 $13.00

Permanent Healing
Dr. Daniel R. Condron   ISBN 0944386-12-1 $13.00

Dreams of the Soul - The Yogi Sutras of Patanjali
Dr. Daniel R. Condron   ISBN 0944386-11-3 $13.00

Kundalini Rising
Mastering Your Creative Energies
Dr. Barbara Condron   ISBN 0944386-13-X $13.00

Upcoming titles...
Atlantis
Spiritual Science of Dreaming
The Tao Te Ching in the Language of Mind
How to Raise an Indigo Child
Mystic Children: The Three New Races

To order write:

School of Metaphysics
World Headquarters
163 Moon Valley Road
Windyville, Missouri 65783   U.S.A.

Enclose a check or money order payable in U.S. funds to SOM with any order. Please include $4.00 for postage and handling of books, $8 for international orders.

A complete catalogue of all book titles, audio lectures and courses, and videos is available upon request.

Visit us on the Internet at *http://www.som.org*
e-mail: som@som.org

About the School of Metaphysics

We invite you to become a special part of our efforts to aid in enhancing and quickening the process of spiritual growth and mental evolution of the people of the world. The School of Metaphysics, a not-for-profit educational and service organization, has been in existence for three decades. During that time, we have taught tens of thousands directly through our course of study in applied metaphysics. We have elevated the awareness of millions through the many services we offer. If you would like to pursue the study of mind and the transformation of Self to a higher level of being and consciousness, you are invited to write to us at the School of Metaphysics World Headquarters in Windyville, Missouri 65783.

The heart of the School of Metaphysics is a four-tiered course of study in mastering consciousness. Lessons introduce you to the Universal Laws and Truths which guide spiritual and physical evolution. Consciousness is explored and developed through mental and spiritual disciplines which enhance your physical life and enrich your soul progression. For every concept there is a means to employ it through developing your own potential. Level One includes concentration, visualization (focused imagery), meditation, and control of life force and creative energies, all foundations for exploring the multidimensional Self.

Experts in the Universal Language of Mind, we teach how to remember and understand the inner communication received through dreams. We are the sponsors of the National Dream Hotline®, an annual educational service offered the last weekend in April. Study centers are located throughout the Midwestern United States. If there is not a center near you, you can receive the first series of lessons through correspondence with a teacher at our headquarters.

For those desiring spiritual renewal, weekends at our Moon Valley Ranch offer calmness and clarity. Full Spectrum™ training is given during these Spiritual Focus Weekends. Each weekend focuses on a ray that corresponds to a level of consciousness, an energy transformer, and a quality of thinking. More than a traditional class or seminar, these gatherings are experiences in multidimensional awareness.

The Universal Hour of Peace was initiated by the School of Metaphysics at noon Universal Time (GMT) on October 24, 1995 in conjunction with the 50th anniversary of the United Nations. We believe that peace on earth is an idea whose time has come. To realize this dream, we invite you to join with others throughout the world by dedicating your thoughts and actions to peace for one hour beginning at 11:30 p.m. on December 31st through 12:30 a.m. January 1st each year. Living peaceably begins by thinking peacefully. We invite SOMA members to convene Circles of Love in their cities during this hour. Please contact us about how you can participate.

There is the opportunity to aid in the growth and fulfillment of our work. Donations supporting the expansion of the School of Metaphysics' efforts are a valuable way for you to aid humanity. As a not-for-profit publishing house, SOM Publishing is dedicated to the continuing publication of research findings that promote peace, understanding and good will for all of Mankind. It is dependent upon the kindness and generosity of sponsors to do so. Authors donate their work and receive no royalties. We have many excellent manuscripts awaiting a benefactor.

One hundred percent of the donations made to the School of Metaphysics are used to expand our services. Donations are being received for Project Octagon, the first educational building on the College of Metaphysics campus. The land for the proposed campus is located in the beautiful Ozark Mountains of Missouri. This proposed multipurpose structure will include an auditorium, classrooms, library and study areas, a cafeteria, and potential living quarters for up to 100 people. We expect to finance this structure through corporate grants and personal endowments. Donations to the School of Metaphysics are tax-exempt under 501(c)(3) of the Internal Revenue Code. We appreciate any contribution you are free to make. With the help of people like you, our dream of a place where anyone desiring Self awareness can receive wholistic education will become a reality.

We send you our Circle of Love.